I0089450

HOW THOUGHTS BECOME THINGS™

BY DOUGLAS VERMEEREN

BASED ON THE FILM FEATURING BOB PROCTOR, DENIS WAITLEY, JOE VITALE, JOHN DEMARTINI, JOHN ASSARAF, MARIE DIAMOND, BOB DOYLE, DOUGLAS VERMEEREN, TRAVIS FOX, MEAGAN FETTES, MARINA BRUNI, JASON PARKER

CREATED BY MAGNIFICENT MOTION PICTURE WORKS
DVD DISTRIBUTION BY WATERSIDE PRODUCTIONS INC.

Copyright © 2021 by Douglas Vermeeren

All rights reserved. This book or any portion thereof
may not be reproduced or used in any manner whatsoever
without the express written permission of the publisher
except for the use of brief quotations in articles and book reviews.

Printed in the United States of America

First Printing, 2021

ISBN-13: 978-1-954968-55-4 print edition
ISBN-13: 978-1-954968-56-1 ebook edition

Waterside Productions

Waterside Productions
2055 Oxford Ave
Cardiff, CA 92007
www.waterside.com

SPECIAL THANKS

There are many people who need to be recognized and thanked for their support in being able to make this project and the film part of this project happen. If there's one thing I've learned in my journey of making these projects, it's that they are really the result of a good team. I have a great team!

Some of the amazing people involved in this project have been with me for all four of my films. They have been superstars. There are literally so many to mention and this page could literally be as long as the scrolling credits from the film. Certainly, you are all so valuable and important. I encourage you as the reader to go and read these credits.

Some that deserve special mention would be my family who was so supportive in the creation of this project. Naturally for anyone reading this who has participated in an entrepreneurial activity such as this, knows that the family of the visionary often has to make significant sacrifices. Mine has had to do that. Holly, Markus, Dez, Christianna - Thank you for your profound support. I love you guys!

I want to thank our publishing team at Waterside Bill Gladstone, Joshua.

I do want to thank Randall who also helped with early work with the manuscript.

I also want to thank the thought leaders who brought their time and expertise to this project. You are all such amazing people and great friends. For most of you, we have collaborated many times over the years, in other movies, books and on stage. I look forward to many more collaborations. I love you all.

I wanted to specifically recognize and say thank you to the following leaders and their teams: Bob Proctor, Denis Waitley, Joe Vitale, John Demartini, John Assaraf, Marie Diamond, Bob Doyle, Travis Fox, Meagan Fettes, Marina Bruni, and Jason Parker.

Some special mentions I'd like to recognize are a few people from my team that have gone above and beyond in the creation of the How Thoughts Become Things Project: Douglas Van Voorst, Jeff Roldan, Emma Wikstrom, Jay Larracas, Eugene, Christopher Michel, Ash Ahern, Jerusalem Alemayehu, Angela Wiseman, Justin Harwood, Ellen Parker, Bob Sumner, Caitlyn Mytopher, Jaclyn Brown, and Marian Clarissa Medina.

I apologize to anyone I may have missed. I really appreciate you for your help in making this happen.

One last person I want to thank:

I want to thank you, the reader. Without your support choosing to learn about this important subject, as well as reading my books and watching the films, we wouldn't be able to create them. I appreciate you and wish you the greatest success.

FOREWORD
By Bob Proctor

Over my more than five decades in the personal development industry, I have encountered thousands upon thousands of people who want to know the secret to success. They're looking for that one nugget of wisdom, complex theory or magic bullet that will make them successful. In reality, the secret is so simple, most people miss it.

Back in the early 60's, the dean of personal development, Earl Nightingale, spoke about "how thoughts become things" in his classic program, The Strangest Secret recording, which went on to become one of Nightingale Conant's flagship programs. He suggested that the secret to success lies in the fact that: we become what we think about.

Throughout history, the really great authors in the field of personal development, James Allen, Wallace D. Wattles, Thomas Troward, Genevieve Behrend, Napoleon Hill, Neville Goddard ... all of them were in complete and unanimous agreement on one thing: our thinking creates our reality or, said another way, thoughts become things.

Animals are totally at home in their environment; they blend in. We are the only creatures on the planet who are not at home in our environment and that is because we have the ability to create our own environment. Our five senses - sight, sound, smell, taste and touch hook us up to our outside world and allow us to navigate that world in a very basic manner. However, what we're not taught is that we also have been gifted with six mental faculties that allow us to tap into our inside world, where our real power lies. These faculties are Memory, Reason, Imagination, Intuition, Reason and Perception.

We have been taught to live from the outside in, allowing our physical results to dictate what we think and ultimately create in our lives, but there's a totally different way to live, one that offers us a totally different pallet from which to create. We have the ability to use our marvelous mind to create the life of our choosing. James Allen said, "We think in pictures, and it comes to pass, environment is but our looking glass."

In his book and film, How Thoughts Become Things, Doug Vermeeren does a great job breaking down the creative process. Virtually everything we see has been created twice: first in the mind of the person who dares to imagine what is possible and then again in the physical creation of the thing imagined.

Regardless of what you have done up until this point in your life, you can do better, much better. I was 26 with no business experience, a series of horrible jobs the length of my arm, no money, a bad attitude, and no hope of change, but I did it! Through the help of a good friend, Ray Stanford, who placed a copy of Napoleon Hill's Think and Grow Rich into my hands, my life spun around on a dime. Ray said to me, "Your way's not working, why don't you try mine?" I thought, what have I got to lose? I've got nowhere to go but up... and up I went!

Ray started me on a path of learning which led to me to meeting and studying with some of the most prolific teachers of my life. Many of these teachers became life-long mentors; I became obsessed with learning. So, if you're reading this and thinking, "Sure, he can, but I can't," let me assure you, you can. This book will get you started.

Through the use of your imagination, you have the power to create anything you want. There are no parameters or limits to your imagination. Through it you're hooked up to the "no thing" where everything is possible. You can tap into universal intelligence to design the life you want, rather than accept a life by default. You can create it as big or as little as we choose. It's your choice.

Now, you can't just think about something once and then BAM, it appears before you. In simple terms, you have to create the image of what you want, then you turn that image over to your sub-conscious mind, you get emotionally involved with it, you take action on it and the action creates a re-action.

You know the movie, The Secret, did as much for the personal development industry as anything I've seen in my lifetime, but, as good as the movie was, I believe it fell short. The movie focused on the Law of Attraction, but as important as that law is, it's a secondary law. The Law of Vibration is the primary law. This law states that nothing rests; everything is in a state of motion – in one form or another. Energy is continually moving into and out of form. Every single thing, seen or unseen, is on a level of frequency. Put yourself on that frequency, and you will have the thing.

In How Thoughts Become Things, you'll learn about the power of choice, the power of your thoughts, the power of perception and beliefs, the power of change, and the power of improvement. You will also learn about how the programs you have believed, and which have been affecting every area of your life up until now are not permanent. You'll also discover how a change in your circumstances is literally only a new thought away, and how quickly the process can occur.

I encourage you to delve into this book. Don't read it as you've been taught to... from cover to cover. No, read it with a view in mind, "How can I use each chapter in this book to cause a positive change in my life." You may never get to the end of the book – that's not the purpose. Apply the material and watch your life grow.

Bob Proctor
Teacher in The Secret and Best-selling author of "You Were Born Rich"

Introduction

"Everything starts in the mind.
Everything starts with a thought."
- Dr. Marina Bruni

Welcome to the book for the film "How Thoughts Become Things." Thank you for joining us. If you've seen the movie, you'll notice very quickly that although this book follows some of the main points of the film, and also shares many of the quotes from the teachers in the film, there are several big differences.

The first is that I have gone deeper into the content we shared in the film in the hopes that you will develop a deeper understanding of the principles and concepts we presented there.

Second, I have introduced some ideas that I really wanted to include in the film but unfortunately, we were just not able to do so, and perhaps most importantly, I have added questions, exercises and applications that will help you use the material from both the book and the film in practical ways in your life in real time.

Important notice: In a recent interview with the media, they asked me about the wonderful cast we have in the film. While sharing who these teachers are and thinking about their accomplishments, I was suddenly and powerfully struck with the thought that they actually aren't the most important people in the film. In fact, if I look at my "why," as to why I made the film and why I do the work, it became clear that the most important cast member in the film is YOU.

The success of the movie and book will be measured by how we can help you achieve the things you are desiring to manifest in your life.

It won't take you long to recognize that "How Thoughts Become Things" is very different than any film or book you've seen up until now. Not only is the information directly practical and easy to implement, but I have specifically sought to include supplemental materials that will allow you to implement the lessons from the project in your life.

Certainly, I hope you have already seen the movie by this point, and if you haven't, I encourage you to go and watch it immediately. When you acquire the movie, you will get a workbook that will guide you through the film. In addition to the workbook, there are several other additional tools such as audios, interviews, video modules and so forth that are accessible in that portal that will make this material so much richer in your life. The behind-the-scenes interviews and tools will allow you to progress quickly into manifesting the things you really want in life.

Each of these materials was designed after careful consideration into how people learn, retain and act on information when they receive it. It could be said that these tools are designed with HOW thoughts really do become things.

This book is also designed the same way. In each of the upcoming chapters I have included exercises, questions and activities that will embed the concepts from this book in your thinking, habits, and daily activities. You will literally see your thinking elevate and your possibilities unfold.

I invite you to use a notebook or journal alongside this book so you can complete the exercises in greater detail and see how your journey is unfolding. I would also invite you to return to the book and these exercises frequently. As you do, you will see in your growth and experience a greater degree of progress. I would recommend that you use this book often until it literally becomes second nature.

In the book, I have also included many of the lessons from the film with direct quotations from the teachers. Naturally, I'm sure you'll agree that the ideas we are teaching have been expressed and articulated by them clearly and with very good examples. There's no need to reinvent the idea. As well, I have included some of my own quotes from the film for the same reason.

There are several quotes from these original interviews that for one reason or another was not able to make it into the completed film. In some ways, this book is not only an expanded version of the principles taught in the film, but it is also an extended version of the film in these regards.

You will also see some ideas appearing that were expressed in my previous films: The Opus, The Gratitude Experiment and The Treasure Map. If you haven't yet seen these films, I would also invite you to check them out. Not only will they help you achieve your success in more effective ways, but each film shares some powerful teachings from several of the world's top thought leaders that you've never heard expressed elsewhere.

The principles from each of these films are like pieces of a puzzle. Together they form an incredible image that gives a more accurate picture of the final result.

So, how did "How Thoughts Become Things" come about?

One of the most common repeated questions interviewers ask me about the film is "how did it come about?" This is an intriguing question that is as interesting as the film itself.

The journey to creating this film began in the fall of 2006. Like most of the world, I was somewhat swept up in the excitement created by the film "The Secret." For me it was particularly interesting as many of the teachers in that film were close friends of mine. Because I was so immersed in teaching these principles and because of my close connection to this world, I had many people asking my opinion on the Law of Attraction.

At the time the term 'Law of Attraction' was new to so many people. While I gave my answers to those who asked, I recognized that what the film "The Secret" had done most of all was start a very new conversation. As much as I was involved in answering questions, I had some of my own.

While thinking about these questions, I happened to be with a highly educated friend of mine. She had degrees in psychology, medicine and an extensive background in neuroscience. I thought, if anyone had an opinion that would be interesting about the Law of Attraction, she would have it. So, I asked her what she thought about all this discussion on the Law of Attraction.

Her answer surprised me. She said, "The Law of Attraction isn't really a law. It's more of a theory." Intrigued, I asked her to explain.

She explained that for something to be considered a scientific law there are several requirements:

1) Scientific law is based on cause and effect.
The Law of Attraction did qualify in this regard. It did produce an outcome.

2) There needs to be variables that can be quantified.
The Law of Attraction struggled in this aspect. It was nearly impossible to place your feelings and focus into quantifiable units. It was also impossible to attach a quantifiable measurement to units of action or specify the kind of action that needed to be undertaken. Considering the law of attraction is so unique to the individual, rarely is it approachable by different people in similar ways.

3) The variables need to produce consistent results when applied by all.
As stated above, with such a spectrum of unique interpretations and experience, there is no standardized approach or results generated with the Law of Attraction at all.

In other words, from a scientific point of view, the Law of Attraction failed the definition of law in 2 out of the 3 criteria.

She then declared that because the law of attraction cannot be measured in these ways that it was more of a theory rather than a law. I was fine with that explanation. However, I did know that although the concept of 'Law of Attraction' was not able to qualify as a law, it still produced incredible results. I had seen it in my own life and the lives of many others.

As I considered the experiences of the teachers in the film, many of whom I had known firsthand for quite some time, I knew that there was something powerful operating with the Law of Attraction. I just didn't know how to describe it.

It was then that I started working on my first film. The film was called "The Opus," with the subtitle, "From Vision, to Plan, to Performance."

My goal in that film was to answer the questions surrounding how to apply the Law of Attraction in real life. The answers I received were incredible. It is for that reason that I recommend you include a viewing of that film as part of your journey to understanding how to use the Law of Attraction to manifest your desires and goals.

However, even though that film gave powerful insights to myself and others, it was the beginning of a journey that led me further down the path of how our thoughts influence our outcomes.

For those familiar with my story and my work, you will know that one of the things I am known for is my interviews with more than 400 of the world's top achievers and business leaders. The media refers to me as the modern-day Napoleon Hill.

The reason I bring up that work is that I wanted it clear that the answers you will find in the pages of this book, and the film, are not just results of interviewing thought leaders in the personal development space, but achievers in a variety of endeavors.

In other words, the information you are about to experience wasn't just from a select group of people that had a vested interested in teaching or sharing the Law of Attraction. I wanted to share experience from people who had achieved high levels of success using these principles in practical terms.

Among those I interviewed were million- and billion-dollar business owners, celebrities who had won Academy Awards, Grammy Awards and international recognition; athletes who had won Olympic medals, played professional sports at high levels and had set incredible world records; Inventors and trailblazers who had created things that either changed our daily lives or created completely new ways of doing things. As I interviewed these people, I released that there was a clear HOW behind thoughts becoming things. In addition, the patterns and path of thoughts manifesting a desired outcome could be replicated and repeated by anyone.

As I searched for these answers, my quest included much from the Law of Attraction discussion, but what surprised me more was how much of modern psychology, neuroscience and studies in human behavior played a big role. One could argue that the research in this film and book are among the most practical and effective tools created thus far to answer these questions.

My goals with this project are enclosed carefully in the title of the film, "How Thoughts Become Things." I will talk in more detail about this further in the book. Naturally, we will talk a lot about "thoughts" and "things," and currently that is where most people spend their time, because people are often preoccupied with their thoughts, usually in the form of what they are struggling with.

Most people spend a lot of time trying to control their thoughts such as, avoiding negative thinking or fighting against fear, trying to stay positive, looking for optimism and experiencing frustration when thoughts of a failed past or a daunting future overtake them.

"Things" are usually what everyone wants and seem to be what people want to figure out how to get. Whether it's wealth, material things, better relationships, the ideal weight, improved feelings of self-worth, or whatever it is they feel they are lacking, this becomes the focus. So, many people invest and inject themselves entirely into the pursuit of these things only to discover that attainment wasn't the real objective after all.

However, I want to point out that the other two words that will most likely be more important to you. When you truly understand their relevance, incredible things will begin to happen in your life. These words are "how" and "become."

"How" refers to: how your thoughts arrive, how they behave when they appear, how you can use the way your brain sorts this information to help you and empower you, and how you separate your thoughts into things that matter and things that are just passing, fleeting thoughts that can't help you or harm you. Most people struggle with understanding this power and as a result struggle with a poor attempt to continually reset their thoughts not realizing this is not the goal.

"Become" is a hidden key. In fact, if you look carefully at the logo designed for this project, you'll notice that I had instructed the designer to make the word slightly smaller. The lesson there is that it is a hidden key.

You've probably heard my friend, Bob Proctor, when talking about the Law of Attraction say that "everything vibrates at a frequency." He has gone on to explain further that if you want to manifest something in your life, you need to vibrate at that same frequency. Well, that is the essence of becoming. To be able to manifest something, you must rise to the frequency of the thing which you wish to manifest.

Let's express this same thought in a layman's terms. Become means change. If you want to have things in your life that you don't currently possess, you must make some changes. I love what the motivational philosopher Jim Rohn once said, "If you win the lottery and want to keep it, you need to learn how to become a millionaire real fast."

Manifesting and maintaining new outcomes in your life requires you to become new as well. This book along with the film will show you how to do that. Be prepared to make changes and you will soon discover changes in the things you attract.

Exercise 1 - Take some time to consider what you really want to manifest in your life. Be specific and describe it in as detailed a way as you can. Now take some time and think of who you would need to become in order to manifest this in your life. What feelings, attributes and habits would support this new reality?

Exercise 1.1 - Observe others who have manifested realities or circumstances you would like to have in your own life. Identify as best as you can what they have felt, believed, or done to create these outcomes.

Questions - Introduction
What was the big question that influenced the film?
Why should you complete the exercises and questions in each chapter?
Who is the most important person in the film?
What are the 3 things required for scientific law?
How is the Law of Attraction more of a theory?
How could you benefit from the Law of Attraction?
Why is it important that these lessons have practical application?
Why is understanding "how" your thoughts become things important?
Why is understanding "become" such a powerful tool in manifesting your thoughts?
How is becoming a hidden key?

HOW THOUGHTS
BECOME THINGS™

What is thought? How is it attached to the reality that you experience?

How is it that some people seem to be master manifesters, immediately creating their dreams and desires, while others seem to struggle and create nothing but frustration and lack? Do your thoughts actually have the power to create your reality? Can thoughts actually become things? If so, how is this all possible?

Thought is like a spark; it initiates the process, like a spark initiates a fire. - Dr. Marina Bruni

The pictures in your mind and the feelings that you hold are the beginning of the reality you experience. The thoughts that produce your reality are your highest power. They are the true power of creation.

We're the only creature on the planet that's totally disoriented in our environment. All the other little creatures are completely at home in their environment; they blend in. We don't. We're totally disoriented and that is because we've been given the godlike ability to create our own environment, and we have higher faculties. - Bob Proctor

Our thoughts are a clear indication that we can create at higher levels than other creatures on the planet. We can form thoughts that utilize our past, the things we have experienced, learned from and observed, to construct a future designed by choice. Unlike so many other organisms on the planet, we have the power to adapt and shape our experience.

The challenge that most people experience begins with the fact that most people do not realize that they have the power to choose what they will create. Most people live their life through default acceptance rather than deliberate activity. When we choose to use our higher faculties deliberately, we are pleasantly surprised that we can shift all things in our existence to a higher form.

When we actually get into the metaphysics and the material part of it, we might forget where the beginning was the beginning when you trace it back. It's your thoughts, your thoughts create reality. - Joe Vitale

Thoughts are the beginning. They are the sparks that ignite the process of creation. Naturally, not all thoughts return as things in your reality, just like some sparks don't create a blazing fire. However, they have the potential to create the fire and often what happens next is the result of the fuel and environment that you add to it.

Your thoughts are the most powerful creative force in the universe; anything that you can think about and think through, you can create. - Douglas Vermeeren

Your thoughts are the most powerful things that you possess when it comes to creating your reality, but most people focus on thoughts and things when it comes to the title "How Thoughts Become Things." The real focus should be on how, which is the process and the things that you have control over. The other word that's important is become. Become refers to the changes that you'll need to make, and who you'll need to become in order to create and maintain the things that you desire most, showing that picture in our mind all the time.

Thinking is the true power of creation, and the problem is most people do not think. If you listen to most people, they never say what they were saying if they were thinking. And if you observe their behavior, they'd never do what they were doing if they were thinking. Although it's the highest function we're capable of, very few people do it. - Bob Proctor

Thinking involves much more than just letting ideas enter your mind. Thought involves a more proactive approach, deciding what you will allow to enter your mind and more specifically what you will choose to do with those thoughts.

Thoughts involve a higher-level evaluation rather than a lower level of acceptance. The more we can understand how our thoughts arrive and the power we have to shape them and label them, the more power we have to create and manifest new realities.

There's a huge difference between having thoughts and thinking. Thinking involves higher cortical functions of our brain, whereas thoughts, they're just there and they're just random. Some make sense, some don't make sense. Our job then is to be aware of the thoughts. Our job is to say, yes, this one serves me and will move me forward towards my goals, my dreams, my vision for my life, or this is a random thought that maybe has some basis in truth and some basis in fantasy. It may be some reconstruction of an experience that I've had in my past or one that I've seen somebody have on TV or heard about on the radio or read about in a book or heard from a family member or a friend. We just make choices, and the only purpose for thoughts are to give us a lot of options. - John Assaraf

Every single thought you're thinking, every word you speak, is like a declaration to the universe. - Jason Parker

Not everything we think is the truth or the reality. Often our unwillingness to investigate or consider our thoughts leaves us with conclusions that are incomplete, unrealistic, and sometimes even unfair to ourselves. We are capable of infinitely more than we realize because we rarely make the effort to consider our thoughts in a more careful way.

Imagine if you had a bingo machine in your head with 50,000 thoughts that just popped up every single second of every day. Do all of those thoughts become things, or are those thoughts just randomly percolating up based on triggers from what you're thinking about or triggers from your outside world, that your brain is percolating up for whatever reason, just in case you might need it? Most of it is not the truth. So, thoughts are not things, thoughts are just thoughts. They are nothing more than little effervescent bubbles of ideas that are percolating from your subconscious mind. Now, if or when we take a thought and we investigate it, is it real or is it not worth pursuing? Is it constructive or destructive? Do we want to take this and do something with it? Do we just allow it to float right by? When we take a thought or an idea that percolates up from our memory bank or our imagination, and then we actively pursue doing something about it, that's when it becomes a thing. - John Assaraf

Even things that haven't been invented yet already have some form of existence. Pause for a moment and observe that the seeds of inspiration that lead to those inventions are all around us. They appear in the form of problems to be solved and solutions that we need. These problems, challenges and questions are ready to whisper to those who will listen. Those who hear these whispers, and think on them with imagination, will become the creators of the inventions we have yet to experience.

Your thoughts are generally a result of stimulus. The thoughts we experience are generally a result of a stimulus in our world. Let me use an example to illustrate this point and we will return to this example later in the book. I want you to read this word:

Dog

As you think about a dog, you may consider the breed of dog, the size, the color, and possibly even the temperament of the dog, but the interesting thing is that until I mentioned the word "dog", most likely you weren't thinking about the animal.

In this way, our thoughts are reactive or responsive to stimuli. Most of the thoughts we have throughout the day respond to things we encounter in our environment just in the way that your thoughts were directed towards the idea of a dog.

However, had I told you in the introduction of the book that sometimes during your reading of this book I would mention the word "dog," you would think about it. However, if you decided ahead of time to make some decisions about the dog, you would be able to be more proactive in your choice. You could have done the pre-work so to speak. You could have built the dog in your mind so that you would have known exactly what the dog would look like. You would also have been able to decide clearly what the dog did not look like. As a result of deciding in advance, you have built a boundary around your ideal dog, and you prevent me from hijacking it in the moment.

Let's now use this analogy to shift into the real world. Everyday around us there are things that will provoke us to think a certain way. For most people, they are on autopilot. They haven't done the pre-work on what they really want. Instead of deciding ahead of time what they would like to create they are continuously in responsive mode as things appear.

They don't know who they want to be in relation to the world around them.
They don't know where they want to put their time and efforts.
They don't know what kinds of relationships they want to create.
They don't have a long-term view of the direction they want their life to take.

Most people live their life from an immediate gratification point of view. You can rest assured that immediate gratification never creates lasting happiness. Recently I was asked on a media interview about my definition of happiness. Many people have expressed that happiness is a choice. I believe that is partially true.

A few years ago, I had a chance to speak at a maximum-security prison in North Carolina. I want to remind you that this was a maximum-security prison. Consider for a moment the characters that would have been there and what you might have to do to merit the maximum-security status. These were not the nicest guys you'd want to meet.

After my talk I had a chance to sit and visit with a few of these men one on one. I'll never forget what one of the inmates said in regards to choice. He said that at the time he was committing the murder he was guilty of, he thought he was making a good choice.

The result was that he had lost his freedom. He hurt his family; he hurt the victim's family, and the victim lost his life. Not all choices create happiness. Happiness is not a choice. I'd like to expand your thinking on this definition of happiness.

Happiness begins with a choice but is complete when our choices create consequences we are pleased with. I might add that any choice which limits our freedom or our ability to choose again is a poor choice.

Back to the idea of our thoughts being influenced by the stimulus in our daily life. We may not be able to control all of the different stimuli we may encounter in a day, but we can certainly make some decisions ahead of time to determine how we will receive the stimuli.

Selection of thoughts

As I mentioned earlier in the book, when the concept of 'How Thoughts Become Things' is shared with most people, they generally focus most on 'things.' They often get excited about the idea or concept of being able to manifest material things into their life.

In my research and experience of working with people, I have found that there are five primary areas of things that people seek or set as goals. I call these the pillar areas:

1) **Self**
2) **Spirituality**
3) **Health**
4) **Relationship**
5) **Abundance**

Let me give a definition of what I mean by each and an exercise that will help you understand your feelings about each. When you do this exercise, you will immediately see how each can be better manifested by creating recognition in your thoughts when certain stimuli arrive in your daily activities.

Exercise - Read and complete the following exercise to give you a better understanding of each of the pillar areas.

1) Self

Self refers primarily to feelings about yourself. Perhaps some of the things you want is a stronger self of self-worth, self-confidence, self- respect and self-empowerment. Naturally you can do the pre-work to identify areas in your day where you have felt robbed of these feelings in the past and make a decision in advance as to how you will interpret or respond to these situations as you encounter the stimulus that is triggering this kind of thinking in the future.

If this is an area where are you are wanting to create new outcomes, please complete the following chart. A past triggering event would be the stimulus that created the past response. By identifying the event and constructing a new response you will have done the rework to be able to have more power to create and manifest new outcomes. (I would encourage you to do this exercise in a spare workbook or journal so that you can return to this book again without being influenced by what you write today.)

Outcome you desire

_____

_____

_____

Past triggering event

_____

_____

_____

Past response

_____

_____

_____

New response

_____

_____

_____

How will you feel with the new consequences that will arrive?

_____

_____

_____

2) Spirituality

Spirituality does not specifically refer to your religion or your beliefs, however it can certainly include those things. A useful way to think about your spirituality is to consider how you operate according to your ethics or beliefs. Do you feel you are living in harmony with your spiritual understanding and connection with others?

Many people measure this in terms of a feeling of peace that they are doing what they know to be right and true.

If this area where are you are wanting to create new outcomes, please complete the following chart. A past triggering event would be the stimulus that created the past response. By identifying the event and constructing a new response you will have done the rework to be able to have more power to create and manifest new outcomes. (I would encourage you to do this exercise in a spare workbook or journal so that you can return to this book again without being influenced by what you write today.)

Outcome you desire

_____

_____

_____

Past triggering event

_____

_____

_____

Past response

_____

_____

_____

New response

_____

_____

_____

How will you feel with the new consequences that will arrive?

_____

_____

_____

3) Health

Health is somewhat a broad category. For some people it speaks directly to a level of fitness, nutrition and even physical appearance. To others it simply represents a reshaping of habits like quit smoking, lose weight or start working out more regularly. As with each of these categories there is no correct or exclusive answer. You may define it in a way that feels right for you.

If this is an area where you are wanting to create new outcomes, please complete the following chart. A past triggering event would be the stimulus that created the past response. By identifying the event and constructing a new response, you will have done the rework to be able to have more power to create and manifest new outcomes. (I would encourage you to do this exercise in a spare workbook or journal so that you can return to this book again without being influenced by what you write today.)

Outcome you desire

_____

_____

_____

Past triggering event

_____

_____

_____

Past response

_____

_____

_____

New response

_____

_____

_____

How will you feel with the new consequences that will arrive?

_____

_____

_____

4) Relationships

Relationships is not just limited to your connection with family members like a parent, spouse, sibling or children. It can certainly be focused on these, and if there are challenges in those relationships at the moment, they are most likely the ones that are at the forefront of your mind. However, this category encompasses all relationships and connections with human beings around you at all levels.

One thing that I think is important to point out is that from a scientific point of view, it has been clearly established, that as an organism, we are highly social. We thrive through cooperation with others; we are validated through others, and we receive our nurturing through others. We need others and how we interact with others is one of the most significant factors that either expands or contracts our feelings of happiness or self-worth.

If this is an area where are you are wanting to create new outcomes, please complete the following chart. A past triggering event would be the stimulus that created the past response. By identifying the event and constructing a new response, you will have done the rework to be able to have more power to create and manifest new outcomes. (I would encourage you to do this exercise in a spare workbook or journal so that you can return to this book again without being influenced by what you write today.)

Outcome you desire

_____

_____

_____

Past triggering event

_____

_____

_____

Past response

_____

_____

_____

New response

_____

_____

_____

How will you feel with the new consequences that will arrive?

_____

_____

_____

5) Abundance

Abundance is one of the most sought after if not the first consideration when the idea of 'things' is discussed. While not everyone rushes in to think about monetary or material things, nearly everyone equates having more in their life with the idea of creating abundance. Whether you define it as time, opportunity, ability, knowledge or money, abundance is about expansion.

You can't expand what you have, until you expand who you are. - Douglas Vermeeren

Abundance is truly all around us and is available to anyone. One of the most challenging aspects for most people is to see the opportunities that will create it and lay the groundwork for it to arrive. (I invite you to get a copy of my book "The Truth About Manifesting Money" to understand how this can easily be corrected and how to start manifesting money in greater quantities.)

If this is an area where are you are wanting to create new outcomes, please complete the following chart. A past triggering event would be the stimulus that created the past response. By identifying the event and constructing a new response, you will have done the rework to be able to have more power to create and manifest new outcomes. (I would encourage you to do this exercise in a spare workbook or journal so that you can return to this book again without being influenced by what you write today.)

Outcome you desire

_____

_____

_____

Past triggering event

_____

_____

_____

Past response

_____

_____

_____

New response

_____

_____

_____

How will you feel with the new consequences that will arrive?

_____

_____

_____

Duality of thoughts

It is not uncommon to hear people talk about overcoming negative thinking in order to manifest the outcomes that they want and desire. In fact, many people that I've spoken with over the years tend to think that the Law of Attraction has a hard time working unless they can control their thoughts to focus only on positive, powerful, empowering or proactive thoughts.

Discouragement and disappointment set in as they quickly discover that it is nearly impossible to keep your thoughts positive and powerful all the time. Perhaps you've had the same experience? Try as you may to stay focused on the best thoughts, negative thoughts or doubts creep in and begin to take over.

This can be quite discouraging. Many of the letters we have received from students and people around the world trying to manifest, center on the plea for help for a strategy to help them control their thinking.

You might be surprised at what we write back. It is the most helpful and supportive advice that we could give when you understand how thoughts really work and how they arrive.

Thoughts are in two parts. They are a duality. Each thought has a positive side and a negative side, and they will always arrive in pairs. In other words, thoughts will have a positive element and a negative element. Let me use an example. Let's say you wanted to start a new business.

The first thought you will have will be positive and supportive. All inspiration and powerful thoughts start this way. You may begin by thinking of all the reasons why you would be successful. You may think of your background, experience, support, funding, knowledge and so forth. All of the reasons why you would be successful come into your mind and you are enthusiastic and hopeful.

However, right behind it, you will have thoughts of doubt, fear, hesitation and apprehension. The thoughts, as to what you lack and what will be missing, attempt to balance out the positive thoughts. It's your mind's way of trying to reign you back in from taking too big of a risk.

The objective of your mind is to keep you in a safe place, and for most people that means doing nothing.

Everything has a positive and a negative polarity. Think of it like the Yin and Yang. They're both complementary and opposite at once. Not only are they both necessary to create the whole, but there's a part of yin in the yang and a part of yang in the yin. They're inextricably connected in a way that one wouldn't make sense without the other. - **Dr. Marina Bruni**

What happens is this thought, which now has a positive and negative charge, now has several options. You can act on the thought, dismiss the thought, or simply hang on to it for a potential future. So, what will you do? What will happen to the thought?

It's because of the duality of our minds that we second-guess ourselves, overthink things, or feel stuck and don't seem able to make a decision. - Dr. Marina Bruni

A good analogy is to consider this thought like a seed, landing in the ground if you will. Depending on the type of soil will determine what will happen next. If the soil is supportive, the seed will gain power. If the soil is not supportive, the seed will wither and die or be postponed.

What is the soil? The soil is a combination of your programming from the past, your current support network, your past experiences, the strength of will power you have built through past experiences, your feelings of self-confidence and self -belief and many other things. In short, your soil is the influences you have brought into your life and what you believe is possible for yourself.

If you have a strong place for the thought seed to land, the positive side of it will receive more power and you may bring the seed into action. If you have a negative place for the seed to land, it will be neglected and ultimately forgotten. It is interesting to point out that the thought was neither good nor bad. It was both. The power of the seed will be created or destroyed based on how it will be received.

It has been interesting to observe over the years that two very capable people could be sitting in the same seminar room and both have a powerful idea to start a business. Yet each one of them will be thinking on the idea differently. One will feel supported and the other will feel challenged. Within a short time, one of them will create something amazing, while the other will have done nothing at all.

What happens if I have a negative thought? In reality, negative thoughts can actually be quite powerful. What do I mean by that? It's because negative thoughts actually tell you exactly what you don't want, and then once you know what you don't want, the key is to make sure you don't stay in that place. - Jason Parker

Exercise - Consider the next inspiring thought that you have. Choose a thought to create something bigger than you've previously done. Take a careful look at how it starts as a positive, empowering and exciting idea. Now observe how quickly a doubting, fearful and challenging thought appears. Decide in that moment to accept only supportive perspectives of the thought and get started doing something about it.

Momentum is one of the fastest ways to shift a negative or doubting thought to a positive thought. It is very difficult for your mind to question a thought while it is in the motion of doing it. Your mind sees that you are committed, and rather than spend effort trying to show you the negative side of the thought, your mind has already been given a separate job. The job of solving the puzzle of how to do it rather than should I do.

Thinking is a deliberate choice which is different than mental activity
As you begin to understand that positive and negative thoughts arrive together, you will understand more carefully that the Law of Attraction is more about making a choice than it is about feeling good thoughts. As a human being you will have positive and negative thoughts, but it is within your power to determine which thoughts you will focus on, get to work on and believe are possible.

Make some choices in advance of how you will respond when the positive and negative thoughts arrive in your life. It will be very clear with the thoughts that are most important to you. The bolder the positive thought, the more glaring the negative thought will be. Remember always that the thought is a reactive instinct, but the labels you give them are the choice. Make a choice to choose what will empower you and ultimately make you happy.

Question - What is thought?
How are your current thoughts shaping your reality?
What do you really want in your life?
How is thought like a spark?
How do thoughts become a burning reality?
How could things be different than they are today?
How are humans a higher form of creation?
How are we different than other forms of creation on the earth?
How are thoughts affected by stimulus?
How can we more carefully consider our thoughts?
How does our pre-work help us manifest what we really want?
How do happiness, choice and consequence work together?
How can we more carefully select our thoughts?
How does pre-work give our thoughts power?
What are the 5 pillar areas?
Which of the 5 pillar areas do you feel you need to work on most today?
How do thoughts have a duality?
Why do negative thoughts follow positive thoughts?
How can you defeat negative thinking?
Why is momentum important in supporting positive thoughts?
What will you choose to do with your thoughts?

HOW
THOUGHTS
BECOME THINGS™

There is a misconception about the connection between your thoughts and the things you experience. Most people think that thoughts are actually bringing these things into existence and for the most part, that's not actually true. Everything that you want or sincerely desire already exists in some form or another. Your thoughts are nearly putting you on the path to those things wherever they currently exist.

We can create at any scale, large or small, the size doesn't really matter. The real question is, do you see it in your mind? Do you see it clear enough to begin the creation process? A vision or goal that is specific and clear becomes attainable, and near. - Douglas Vermeeren

Thoughts
The topic of thought is spoken of widely and regularly. Most of that conversation focuses around over-coming negative thinking, fears, doubt and similar obstacles. Rarely do we hear of people who recognize that they have the power to change their thinking or that their thinking is the seed that is directly creating the outcome.

The conversation rarely strays from a discussion on how to control thoughts and the bad ones. However, the conversation is much broader than this, and soon you will learn, controlling thoughts is not exclusively an inside job.

Things
The other component of the conversation of is things. In fact, most often this is where people direct their comments. They are intensely focused on the things that they want more than the route to manifest them. It's almost as if people expect or hope these things will arrive like a winning lottery ticket; simply give the universe your shopping list then grab a seat on the couch and watch everything arrive. If you haven't discovered this already, you'll find that this approach will not work. The things that we want, have a beginning which is thought, but the thought is the beginning.

It began as a thought. I don't care if you wanted a car, you wanted the house, you wanted a relationship, you wanted better health, you wanted spiritual awakening. I don't care what it is you want, a movement to end war. I don't know what might come to mind, but the idea is, it begins with a thought. So, the correlation is, thought will lead to concrete reality. - Joe Vitale

Our thoughts are directly connected to our outcomes. However, most people have never made the effort to carefully consider the correlation. Most of the time the things that we want are available all around us and are more accessible than we may have imagined. Unfortunately, most people do not pay attention enough to recognize them in their environment.

Attention is focused on reality rather than possibility. Both can be clear in our vision, and we take action to create the things we see. If we don't see it as a possibility, it's almost as if it didn't exist at all.

More often than not, we'll say "I'd always like to have that" or "I'd like to have this," but we really don't pay attention to it. Then, when it shows up, the first thing is that fraud comes up that says, "well you know that's only for the lucky people," "that's only for the people who know what's really going on," "they know how to run their mind," or "they know the secrets." Well, a secret is, you're never disconnected. The question is, "are you really willing to connect on the

inside and direct your thoughts to what you want so that they line up with what's already out there on the outside?" - Travis Fox

An interesting reality that most people don't consider when it comes to things is that everything you want, already exists in some form or another. What good news that you don't have to create something *Ex Nihilo. Ex Nihilo* is the Latin phrase sometimes used to express the creation of the universe out of nothing.

Whether you believe that the universe came from nothing or not, one thing is certain that everything that you want already exists. This is wonderful news. This means is that everything you want is available. It can become yours. It isn't as much of a matter of creation as it is relocation.

If you want a sports car, it is not an exercise of acquiring the materials, refining them, shaping them, and then assembling them into a car. Others with specific skills have done that for you. Your job is much easier and when we admit that, creation and manifestation using the Law of Attraction becomes easier. It is easier because we can immediately see that everything we want to have manifested exists, and others have helped us. We are not alone in the manifestation process.

Nothing is created or destroyed. If nothing is created or destroyed, everything is already here. It's not a matter of getting. It's a matter of tuning into what's already here. - Bob Proctor

Tuning into the vibrational frequency of what already exists is something that many people have misunderstood. They limit the idea of adjusting your frequency to thoughts, feelings and desires. Those things are just the beginning. Truly shifting your vibration can be found by taking action and shifting your beliefs and activities to be fully supportive in manifesting what you want to arrive in your life. You must become fully invested through everything you think and do.

A great example of being "all in" is found in the idea that you can't manifest abundance if you've got one foot in abundance and the other in scarcity and hope to manifest abundance. You must be all in with your thoughts, words, beliefs, actions and commitments.

Exercise - Consider some of the things you have tried to manifest in your life in the past. In what ways have you let a lack of focus and commitment take away your ability to manifest outcomes and realities that you have desired. Take a moment to identify where things have been divided. If you can repair these divisions, you are on your way to a positive manifestation experience.

Everything that exists and ever will exist already exists. The question is this, "Are you tuning your thoughts into what is already there so you can create it in your life?" - Douglas Vermeeren

When we recognize that the things you want in your life already exist in some form or some place, already we can begin to develop a belief that they are ready and waiting for us. Rather than attempting to create the thing out of thin air, it is more that we are on a quest to find the path between where we are and where the object is. This feels much more believable, and it is something that our thoughts can work with.

I like the way the Maharaja put it. I heard a story. I don't know if it's true, but when he was deciding to take Transcendental Meditation to the world, one of his key people said, "It's going to cost a lot of money. Where's the money going to come from?" He said, "Wherever it is right now," and of course he was telling the truth, because that's where the money always comes from. Wherever it is right now. You've got to attract it. - Bob Proctor

Attraction is a misunderstood concept, as stated above and is worth pointing out again. Attraction and manifestation are not exclusively mental processes. Although they begin in the mind, true attraction involves doing everything in your power to create circumstances where what you want to receive can arrive.

What can you do right now that would help the outcomes you are seeking to become yours?

Speaking about money and abundance, one of my mentors put it this way. He said, "They're always printing money at the mint every single day. They don't stop, and you get to decide how much of it will come into your life." - Douglas Vermeeren

How
Perhaps one of the better descriptions of HOW outlines what you can do to have what you want to arrive. In other words, this is the part of attraction that goes beyond the thinking. How do your thoughts generate the power needed to produce a new reality? What are the strategies that are required?

Become
This is probably the most important word in the title of the film. It refers to the changes that you will have to make in order to manifest the reality and the outcomes that you desire in your life. Jim Rohn once said, "If you win a million dollars in the lottery and you want to keep it, then you need to learn how to become a millionaire very quickly."

The power of manifestation and maintenance comes with what we will choose to become.

The reality of anything we gain in our results and outcomes is that it arrives first through who we become, which affects what we will do and ultimately that translates into what we will have.

Be - Do - Have

What we think about inside, is directly connected to what will occur in our reality outside. Most people are not authentically connected to the things they truly want, so they never manifest the things that will make them happy and fulfilled.

When we try to connect with things that are not in line with our highest values, we will always struggle to manifest them. When we connect to those things that are authentic to us and in line with our greatest values, we don't have to work very hard to start seeing results.

The Things Our Thoughts Create Affect Others
The thoughts we have affect others. They can feel the energy of our thoughts. Have you ever observed someone who is actually thinking happy, positive and empowering thoughts? Even from a distance you

can see that they are happy, and close up, you can see the confidence and kindness in their face. They are literally broadcasting what they think about to the world and others in their body language and their expression. The opposite is also true. When someone is thinking negatively, you see this in their body language too, and certainly their expression will reflect those same thoughts.

The creations of our mind are like a virus affecting everyone we meet. With scarcity thinking, you will not only attract scarcity from the universe, but you will also get it from those you come in contact with as well.

All negative feelings and emotions such as fear, panic, doubt, jealousy and criticism all spread this way, but the opposite is also true. Joy, happiness, power, enthusiasm and abundance all spread the same way. We are not just connected to things but people too!

When it comes to scarcity thinking, not only do we have to be aware of what we are sending out and receiving from others, but it is important that we realize that it is that awareness that protects us from these negative influences. When we are aware, we are in control of how we will participate in the energy of the thinking around us.

The esoteric internet says that we're all connected. You can use the collective unconscious. We're all connected to the collective unconscious. When we send a signal through that, it touches the people that are involved with the only way the signal gets through. It needs a kind of electricity. That electricity is the vibration you create through your thinking that gets evaluated through your physical body. The esoteric body goes out into the world and touches those that are relevant and needed to the completion of whatever the goal is or the intention is for you. - Dr. Joe Vitale

Just imagine, when you speak, it's like a balloon. The moment you have stopped thinking or speaking, the balloon is released. The balloon will arrive through the Law of Attraction to the person that the thought is meant for. - Marie Diamond

Perhaps you've felt the thoughts others have had about you or about something you've said. They haven't spoken a word, but you can sense that they either had good thoughts about you or unpleasant ones. Sometimes those thoughts have been so powerful that they influenced your behavior or your feelings about yourself.

You can pick up the thoughts of somebody on the other side of the world because there is no other side of the world. That's an illusion. There's no space. It's like when you take a picture of some-body with your phone and hit send, they get it instantly. - Bob Proctor

We are all connected, and the energy associated with the dominant thoughts flare. Groups of people can create powerful positive experiences on one hand, and panic and extreme fear or prejudices on the other. As I write this book, the world is in the thick of the COVID-19 pandemic. We have seen how the thoughts of masses have results in group activities that have created global consequences. Some of these consequences have been strongly based in fear and negativity. Others have created positive mes-sages of hope and power. Which side are you on?

When somebody does a blessing in certain rituals, certain religions or cultures. They do blessing, just even think about the wedding blessing. Right. Is that just a priest or the minister that has a blessing of the couple that's getting married but it's like all the friends and family they've come together, there actually are blessing that couple. Yeah. Can you imagine that perhaps the priest or minister is doing a blessing but half of the people in the church or in the ritual are thinking negative about the couple. - Marie Diamond

How marvelous it would be if we all started looking for ways to bless each other! How incredible it would be if we all learned to celebrate the accomplishments and good desires of others. If we all supported each other, good things would arrive more abundantly for all people. Not only would great things arrive for others, but they would arrive for you as well. You would literally be enveloped by abundance as a creator, supporter and a participant. I challenge you to become part of the movement to create abundance and kindness for all.

Second by second, your brain is changing. It's impossible not to have changes in the brain. - Dr. John Demartini

Change is an important principle in progress and achievement. In order to expand what we have, we must first begin by expanding who we are. Starting with ourselves means starting with the things we have control over. When we change ourselves from the inside out, the world we experience outside follows.

With every perception and every associated thought, you change your nervous system, your brain, and the neurotransmitters in neuromodulators, the neural hormones and neuro regulators, which affect the soul walls and their receptors, which then affect the messengers, then the cascading enzymes, and then the genes themselves through epigenetics. You cannot think about something without changing your physiology, and your physiology assists you in the world in creating what your inner most dominant thought desires. - Dr. John Demartini

Our thoughts and our actions always follow our inner most dominant thoughts and values. We may temporarily get started pursuing things we think we should do or be because of the influence of others, but in reality, we will only do that with a halfhearted effort and for a short period of time. We can only truly create according to what we value most.

The good news is that as we become aware of how our current values and beliefs serve us, or don't serve us, we can question them. We can evaluate if they are leading us to where we really want to finish up. We can analyze to see if they are serving us in creating who we want to become, and if they are not, we can change our thoughts, our choices, our responses, our activities and everything else.

The amazing thing that science has proven is that even the very composition and structure of our brain can change. Perhaps you've heard the saying that you can't teach an old dog new tricks. The truth is you can teach anyone new tricks if they are willing to receive it, and the good news is that it happens faster than we've ever believed possible.

Some people will say, you can never change, or you can never think you can ever change. Your thoughts will never change your mindset. I believe every day is a new universe. Every day! - Marie Diamond

Every day is a new universe. It is a new opportunity to create or expand who you are. Every new day is an opportunity to become more aware and realign with the things you truly want and value most. How are you using your new day? Are you giving yourself the opportunity to make the changes that you need to in order to feel good about yourself and your situation? Are you giving yourself permission to let go of what you created in the past to move on to create new outcomes that serve you better?

Change is one of the most significant considerations when manifesting or attracting new outcomes. We must be willing to rise to new levels of thinking and being if we are to improve the things we wish to attract. Attraction is not accidental and until we change our thinking, we cannot change our results. A final note on change that I believe is very important to consider is how it affects our connection and relationship with other people. It's important to remember that everyone is on a journey to create a better future. Improvement is our nature as human beings.

While some people may seem to be getting there faster or with more efficiency, we should keep in mind that everyone is trying to do their best with what they understand. How amazing it would be if we could learn to have more mercy and kindness towards everyone on their personal journeys. How incredible it would be if we could all become kinder and more supportive. A sign of a truly enlightened and abundant individual can be seen in how they treat others. How will you respond to those around you, who just like you are trying to figure things out?

Questions - How thoughts become things
How do our thoughts affect others?
What is the way we attract new things into our life?
How do things that haven't yet been invented, already exist?
Can people change?
What about them can change?
Can we change?
What about us can change?
How does it happen?
How are you responding to others around you?
Are you willing to let go of the old to create something new?
How is everyday a new universe?

HOW
THOUGHTS
BECOME THINGS™

YOU HAVE BEEN PROGRAMMED

When we think about programming, there may be quite a few different things that come to your mind. Typically, most people think of programming as unavoidable patterns and behaviors that have been created within us during our early years. While all of us have been programmed in our past, we are also being programmed right now.

According to some people, your programming not only began at birth but started centuries before. Some people say that our programming rests in our spirits and in our genetics. The very thoughts of your ancestors helped to create the environment and programming we were born into, influencing our belief systems, our values, and the things we believe are possible. Programming creates stories, interpretations, and perceptions.

Reality is based on perception because we've been programmed to see things the way we see them. We don't see with our eyes; we see through our eyes. We see according to the way our programming is. - Bob Proctor

If you happen to think that the world is a messy, desperate, despondent place, you will look into the world, and you will find evidence to match your belief. You'll have your reality match your mindset. Change your mindset, think a different reality. - Joe Vitale

What you believe to be true is true for you. It's not necessarily based on reality. - Jason Parker

Reality is our interpretation of the facts and is in a constant state of construction in our mind. It is a personal affair. Two individuals can experience the same situations and label them very differently.

Our interpretation is a result of what most people call, "our programming." In short, our programming has been built by structures and supports around us. Those structures and supports have built our beliefs, expectations, and perceptions. These are three elements are primarily what determine the meaning we give to the events and circumstances we experience.

All reality is virtual reality. In other words, reality is different for every human being because reality is based on what we perceive, that we've heard secondhand from our family, that we've learned from our environment, and what it means to us. So reality means nothing except for your experience with it. - Denis Waitley

Every time we engage in an activity, even when we stand still, we perceive information and data. As humans, we have this brain that is constantly processing input and data, and our mind learns to make meaning out of all of it. - Dr. Marina Bruni

Throughout our lives and our upbringing, we are programmed and indoctrinated to believe that change needs to be hard. Does it? The answer is no. - Jason Parker

Most people think about the concept of programming, and they think that their programming primarily took place when they were a child. In fact, many studies point to the early childhood ages and suggest that the bulk of your programming is complete by the age of 5. While there is no disputing that many of the tools that we use to build our beliefs are in place by then, this idea of childhood programming is misleading.

Evidence suggests that rather than programming being primarily a childhood function, it is actually on-going. Our programming is currently happening. In fact, even as you are reading this book or watching the film, your programming is being reshaped by the ideas and concepts you are encountering.

Our programming is currently happening. In fact, even as you are reading this book or watching the film, your programming is being reshaped by the ideas and concepts you are coming into contact with.

All of this data becomes a thought. We look at something; we interpret it. We smell it; we hear it; we use all of our senses to combine it, reference all of our experience, and then we have a thought, an idea. Something just occurs to us in our brain, and it happens all the time. Every moment of the day. We're having these thoughts, these reactions to the input of our environment. - Bob Doyle

One of the functions of programming is to hunt for information or evidence that supports beliefs you already have in place. In other words, the stories you place on reality are directed to making you correct. Rather than serving you to find out what is right, your mind seeks to make you right. Naturally this quest to be correct can often cause us to believe false information or skew information to keep patterns that are comfortable but not progressive.

I have this little robot that goes around with me. I tell him what I'm thinking. I'm telling him what I see, and I tell my little robot all my hopes and fears. He listens and remembers everything he hears. At first, my little robot is following my command, but after years of training, he's gotten out of hand. He doesn't care what's right or wrong, or what is false or true, no matter what I try, now he tells me what to do. - Denis Waitley

When we don't question our programming, we follow the commands that our subconscious mind gives to us. Like what Denis Waitley said above, our subconscious mind is like a robot that takes over our ability to choose. We simply obey the commands given to us, and as you can imagine, the robot strives for efficiency and keeps us doing the same things over and over again.

We have over 50,000 thoughts that percolate up from our subconscious minds, based on the patterns that are the trillions of neural connections. Every book we've read, every movie we've seen, every interaction we've had, every experience that we've had, every idea, emotion, sensation that has been orchestrated and organized in our brains, specifically our subconscious brain and our memory center, is percolating up these unimaginable thoughts, some good, some bad, some constructive, some disruptive. Some are worthwhile of our attention, and some are not. - John Assaraf

We are born, and we're just this open book. Our computer, our hard drive, is completely empty, and we start taking input from our parents and our society and our friends. As we grow up, we don't know as children that we can discern; we don't know how to evaluate what's being told to us; it just gets in there, and we are saying yes to everything. Yes, this is hard to do, yet this is easy to do, yes this is possible for me. Yes, money is evil. Whatever it is that we are taught, we have no other reason, we don't know how to evaluate so we just believe it, that becomes our wiring, literal neuropathways in our brain. It just gets stronger with repetitive thought, and we are attracting this evidence as we are doing this, that this thought is real. We get encouragement over and over. Yet, your thoughts are right, your thoughts are correct, and every time we have that thought, wiring gets more, we get stronger and stronger and stronger till we become conscious of the fact that we are wired. That is how that's going to shape our entire experience of reality. - Bob Doyle

Repetitive thoughts that are not evaluated or considered are dangerous. They are dangerous in the sense that they keep us from progressing or realizing our potential. Without evaluating our thoughts, we accept what we have been told to accept as reality. As we operate with these beliefs, they get stronger and more influential until they become the key guiding factors in our life.

When we first start getting programmed, it isn't necessarily through language, because we don't really understand language. We understand through feelings, through what our eyes see and what our ears hear, its tones and sounds, and we pick up that vibrational experience. Before you know it, that vibration starts to develop what's called a feeling or emotion, and we start to program that by pushing those feelings up into the subconscious mind. Then the subconscious, you know, like a big recorder, just records everything from the moment that it occurs all the way until your death. - Travis Fox

Programming happens primarily through our feelings. What is most curious about this is that feelings can often be misinterpreted and meanings that are intended by loved ones can even be misunderstood. As feelings and emotions are constantly occurring within us, we operate more in a response mode to feelings than we do in relation to logical thought.

An important shift might be to spend more time considering how you want to feel, rather than responding to what you currently feel. As you shift more towards your desired feelings, you will begin to see that your thoughts and ultimately your outcomes will follow.

The Dangerous Autopilot

As most people don't question their feelings or their thoughts, they are generally on autopilot or responsive mode. They don't question or consider their thoughts or their feelings.

If something happens that makes them happy, they are happy. If something happens that makes them sad, they become sad. If something provokes them to feel angry, they become angry. They have given away all of their power to choose outside sources.

Even just the terms 'auto' and 'pilot' are worth considering. The term pilot means to direct or control the direction that an object is travelling. Consider for example an airplane. The pilot directs the destination to which the airplane will travel, and it recorrects the trajectory of the airplane if it begins to go off course.

Auto or autopilot is the act of giving up that control or surrendering it to a force or power other than your own.

While going on autopilot is unfortunately a very, very common thing, especially in the western culture, everything is running around very fast. The risk there is when you're going on autopilot means that you are not present in this very moment. - Marina Bruni

The idea of autopilot being a state in which you are not present is very accurate. Autopilot occurs most frequently when we surrender our consideration of the present. It often comes in extreme moments where we feel rushed or relaxed moments where we get lazy. Autopilot occurs as our brain seeks for a way to more efficiently navigate things that are familiar to us.

In this state, we surrender our analytical mind. We proceed without questions or considering what is actually occurring. We literally give up the controls of our airplane and relinquish our control of the direction or destination we are heading to. When we surrender the control, we surrender the flight pattern. Where we will end up is anyone's guess.

Most people on the planet are running on complete autopilot. They're not dreaming big. Maybe they're not at the bottom of the gutter. They're just living their lives because of their wiring. So, everything's just kind of on neutral. They don't dare dream too big, and they're not doom and gloom either, but they're also not realizing their full potential. - Bob Doyle

90% of people or more, keep getting the same results, year after year after year. They're God's highest form of creation, and it looks like they are living like their pets. Just the same results over and over and over again, and there's no need for it. - Bob Proctor

As humans, there will be times that autopilot will be inevitable. Our mind does require moments of autopilot to recharge and configure. However, if we deliberately program our autopilot in advance to stay on course and seek the outcomes we desire, the states of autopilot can become more productive and supportive.

Awareness & Becoming
Our awareness is what gives us the power of choice. The more aware we become of what is entering our thoughts, the more we can challenge our programming to begin attracting more of what we really want through choice rather than floating along by default.

We have in our brain a hierarchical structure, and the forebrain has what is called the medial prefrontal cortex, but that area of the forebrain is the executive center. When we think from our executive center, when we live by highest priorities in life, we start to think in terms of objective goals, which are more even minded, more balanced of an outcome. But we're in our amygdala, which is the more primitive part of our brain, the more hindbrain oriented. We tend to think of only polarized thoughts, one side, which then automatically, intuitively, brings up the other thought to try to balance it. So, we set up a balanced thought, and we strategically plan our objectives, we increase the probability of achieving what is in our most dominant thought. - John Demartini

Clarity and Repetition
The brain is an incredible series of highways, freeways, toll-roads, cul-de-sacs, and construction sites. So, I call these the freeways of the brain, and thoughts are traffic.
- Denis Waitely

Everything that you can think of, everything you've ever thought, everything you've ever seen, all the stuff you've forgotten, it's all there in your subconscious mind. The subconscious mind responds to emotion, and it responds to repetition, and it responds to imagery. So, you create an image, what you would like to have, do or be, and you repeat it, and you repeat it with some sort of emotion, it will go into the subconscious mind, and give it an order to create something that you would like to have, do or be in your life. - Joe Vitale

Authenticity
Authenticity is an important factor when it comes to manifesting the reality you desire.

Authentic expression always supports your highest values. In other words, the activities you choose to do or not do will always support your highest values. If you don't see a connection in the activities you are asked to do with the values you have, you will hesitate, investigate, procrastinate and avoid them at all costs.

One of the primary reasons why people struggle to create new outcomes for themselves is that they can't see how the activities that bridge from where they are now to those desired outcomes fit with their highest values.

You need congruency. You need coherence. You need heart coherence and brain coherence. Together. - Dr. Marina Bruni

A friend of mine said it this way in reference to the rich, but it could literally be true for any outcome you want to create.

Rich people do what's hard so they can live a life that's easy. Broke people do what's easy and as a result get a life that's hard.

The reasons why it becomes hard for most people is that either they never make the connection between what they need to do and what they truly value or they really don't value the outcome.

When you compare yourself to others, you'll inject the values of others into your life, and you'll try to be somebody you're not. That is, you know, authenticity stops you from shining the magnificence. So, this is basically setting out the thoughts that are truly congruent with who you truly are, and thinking about the way you would have your life, not the way other people want you to happen. - Dr. John Demartini

I think before we get into thought, we have to ask, who am I? You know, where did I come from, how do I get here, and we're going to see that. Almost all of our beliefs are ridiculous. - Bob Proctor

Your Programing Is Ongoing
Many are quick to suggest that who you are is a result of programing that happened to you when you were a child, and as a result of circumstances, you were involved in growing up. While these situations have been demonstrated to have a high impact on the beliefs and values you possess, the idea of programming being a childhood experience isn't completely true.

You've most likely heard the saying that you become like the 5 people you spend the most time with. The word 'spend,' points to the present, not some distant time that has vanished away decades ago. The truth is that you are currently being programmed by the people and things you choose to spend your time with now.

Our inside world and our outside world are always connected. The question is where we ask our-selves to disconnect, and that's what social media and tv really do, they take us to another world. Then, we start doing compare and contrast models with ourselves. Am I good enough? Is that successful? Am I tall enough? Am I pretty enough? Am I smart enough, am I educated enough. Do I have enough money? Do I have enough follower? How many subscribers? Here's the thing, if all of that was real, every single person on the planet would be doing it, and then we'd be doing it authentically. Why? Because the people on social media, want to portray a certain image of themselves, and at the moment they're portraying that image, you perceive them that way. You can follow or subscribe, but that doesn't mean that's who they really are, and it has very little to do with you because again, they're showing a perception. You're then perceiving that perception with your own filters and next thing you know, there's this third world that's been created--their invitation, your perception, and now you're over here. We're so disconnected from what's authen-tically ourselves. We can't see the forest through the trees. - Travis Fox

Your environment is like a three-dimensional vision board. - Marie Diamond

What we choose to surround ourselves with has an important influence on our thinking. No doubt you've experienced an inspiring view or been in an environment which made you feel fulfilled. Natu-rally, you've also experienced the opposite as well.

Too often, people discount the importance their environment can have on how they think.

In addition to the actual location, the level of cleanliness or organization in an area also has a bearing on your thinking. Chaos and confusion only create more of the same. Studies have demonstrated that clarity and order expand thinking into more creative and effective ways.

A recent study revealed that students placed in a calm and clean setting had an increase in their abil-ity to solve problems faster and with more effectiveness, while those placed in the opposite environ-ment of chaos and disarray struggled to find more clarity of thought.

Thoughts don't just follow the physical tangible environment, but they also are heavily influenced by what we absorb through sound. It certainly comes as no surprise that music guides our thoughts and emotions.

Think back to a recent time when you were driving your car and one of your favorite songs came on the radio. Not only did your thoughts shift but your behavior followed as you started singing along. It's almost as if you can't help it.

Our environment and the things we bring into it similarly have a way of hijacking our feelings and sometimes our actions.

Exercise - Identify music that makes you feel inspired, uplifted and powerful. Create a playlist that you can include regularly in your day to help lift you to higher levels of thinking and inspiration.

There's a significant scientific basis and evidence that suggests that a calm, clear and organized environment, creates better thought energy, stronger problem solving ability and a higher functioning for all personality types, and the universe won't bless you with more unless you can demonstrate that you can take care of what you have. - Bob Proctor

Everything affects our thinking. I tell people, turn off the mainstream news; it's affecting your thinking. Pay attention to the music you're listening to, pay attention to the movies you're watching, the television you're watching, and pay attention to the social media you are on. Pay attention to how you feel when you are interacting with all these different people and things. If they feel like they're bringing you down, then your vibration is lower and subconsciously your thoughts are being contaminated. You must really become sensitive to all the information that's in your aura and make sure it's as clean as possible. Protect yourself. - Joe Vitale

TV and it's sibling, social media, are the best hypnotist on the planet. - Travis Fox

Most people are like thermometers, and here's what I mean. Everything is external. They get their cue from the market, from the media, from the news, from the catastrophes, and everything is outside influence and therefore they feel that they're totally influenced by what happens outside of them. The truth is, you're a thermostat, what you get is what you said. You raise the level of the image of yourself, your self-awareness. Instead of looking outside for outside influence, look inside. Human nature is reactive. We watch other people first, we watch role models, and we're so desperate to belong. We're so desperate to be included. That is when in Rome, do as the Romans do. Be part of the group, the contagion, the crowd, the rock concert, the end group, the smooth guys, the tough guys. So, we do things that other people do, so that they will include us. Status with peer group, status with experts, being a good competitor, having external things and being powerful, we all seem to want the things that other people have, so that we will be included, and therefore we will be liked. - Denis Waitley

Our thoughts are extremely reactionary and attached to our feelings. We are constantly seeking ways to feel good. One of the ways we do this is to seek out the approval and appreciation of others. As a result, we often surrender our best judgement or our ideal goals in order to feel a positive connection with other people.

We allow our sense of validation and value to come from external sources, but the people around us are generally the most powerful influencing factor that we will bend towards. As humans we are social creatures, and this bending to influence is not a bad thing. However, most people never consider or select a higher level of peer group to be influenced by. One thing all of us want in life is validation and acceptance.

Exercise - Consider your current peer group. Who are you really spending the most time with and whose values are you really embracing and trying to measure yourself against?

Time and Admiration

You've no doubt heard that we become like the 5 people we spend the most time with. We have talked about that concept elsewhere in the book. Certainly, spending time with people is a significant factor to recognizing how we are influenced, but it's not just the time with them that influence's us.

What we admire, we emulate. Those that we admire often have a stronger influence on us more so than those we spend our time with.

Network = Net Values

Our thoughts and feelings are influenced by those we hold in high regard. We will rise to the standards or expectations of those we value, and we will allow those expectations to contribute to the expectations we have on ourselves.

It is our programming that dictates how we interpret the things we experience currently. Because of this programming, we are operating most of the time in a reactive state of mind rather than a proactive state of mind.

Up until now, your programming has determined how the interactions you have with the world around you find place in your conscious mind and how they will be received or acted upon.

Questions - You have been programmed
Where did your existing programming come from?
How are you currently being programmed today?
What are you allowing to influence you right now?
How does awareness help you take better control of your choices in programming?
What is autopilot?
How does autopilot work against us?
How can we deliberately program our autopilot to serve us?
What influences in your environment are currently shaping your thinking?
Who do we seek to emulate?
What is it about them that we admire?
How does our network determine our net values?

HOW
THOUGHTS
BECOME THINGS™

People live in a reactive state rather than a creative responsive state because of survival. They're wired to be that way. We are wired to stay alive. There's a part of our brain that is on alert right now to find out what the threats are, and no matter what's going on, no matter what's being said, we react to it because it's a biological response, but here's the kicker. We want to awaken from that. I think life is all about awakening. We want to awaken from that and be at choice. We want to realize something that's scary or dangerous to our survival and something that we can dismiss--it's not really real at all--and go on and create what we really want to have in life. So, it's all about awakening to what's real. - Dr. Joe Vitale

Happiness, choice, and consequence are a very powerful triad. If used well, they can really help you with your manifesting process. - Dr. Marina Bruni

Choice is the first power we have. Too often people take it for granted and that is what keeps them, repeating the same thoughts they have been circling through in their life. When we recognize that our power really begins when we make a choice to think differently, amazing things can happen.

Within each person is the ability to select new thoughts and new outcomes. Everything that you want is as close as making a decision to change your choices. People can change. Thoughts can change. Outcomes can change.

Most people have not taken the time or made the effort to question their choices and thoughts, up until now. Whatever your circumstances may be or whatever you may be experiencing right now, the one power that cannot be taken from you is the power of choice.

Exercise - Think about a circumstance in your life that you're not happy with. What choices do you have surrounding this choice? How could you choose to think, believe or even act differently than what you are currently thinking, believing or doing about this situation? Is there a more empowered way that you could approach this situation? How would this new choice change the outcome?

Our job is to say, yes, this thought serves me and will move me forward towards my goals and my dreams. This is the thing I want to trade my life for. - John Assaraf

The concept of making a trade is an interesting one. Often, we hear many of the gurus of today suggest that you can have everything you want. You don't need to make a choice between two things. The truth is that often you do have to make a choice. You can't create true focus by trying to capture everything.

In reality, you can't be at two places at once. You can't create something of significance if you are split between two possible outcomes or conflicting desires. Focus and commitment are prerequisites to creation. A simple analogy may illustrate:

Imagine you are in a car driving down the road. If you want to turn both right and left at the same time, what will happen? How can you make this happen? You can't technically turn your steering wheel both right and left at the same time. You will ultimately have to make a choice as to which direction is more important to you, or you will have to remain neutral.

Most people freeze in the neutral position, and as a result, they make no progress towards creating the life they really want.

Exercise - Think about your approach to creating the outcomes you have desired in the past. In what ways have you been holding back your commitment to get committed, focused and on purpose? In what ways have you held back your best efforts with what you wanted most because you wanted to preserve something else that you also wanted? Which outcome was more important to you and why? Take some time to consider the long-term consequences of each outcome and how each would support your values and desires. Now, make a decision to get committed to the outcome that will give you more joy. Then get started taking action to make this chosen outcome a reality!

Awareness proceeds choice. When we become aware that that set of thinking, feelings or actions is not serving us, we are then able to make new choices that will activate new outcomes.

When the thought enters your awareness, you now have free will. What do you do with the thought? You can act on it, or you can let it go. You can let it ride, or you can pass. This is where you get to choose. - Dr. Joe Vitale

And choose you must! There is a power in making a choice. Up until the moment you decide to make a choice, your mental energy is focused on keeping you sitting on the fence balanced between two options. Perhaps you have experienced this where your mind explores the two options, waffling back and forth between the ideas with no commitment or activity.

However, the moment you make a choice and select one of the options as the path you will pursue, your mind shifts into a new gear. Now your mind begins to assemble how you can take action to get started filling the gap between where you are now and the outcome you want to achieve.

Most people never make the choice and spend a lifetime waffling between several half-hearted commitments that they find interesting.

Recently I met a man at one of my Personal Power Mastery seminars. He was 73 years old and quite depressed. As I got to know him, he expressed that he knew where his depression came from. As a young man he had aspirations to be a successful business owner, but also an actor in the theater. Both dreams had him very excited, but he never fully committed to either.

He would start a business and run it for a few months, but as soon as he began to experience success, he would feel a longing to get back on stage as an actor instead of behind a desk. He would then go and take acting classes, spend time at auditions and his business would suffer. Then he would drop the acting and rush back to rescue his business.

Now, he was 73 feeling that his life had slipped away without accomplishing either of his dreams to any significant degree. As we talked about his feelings, he recognized that his feelings were directly linked to his desire to keep from making a choice. He wanted the security of his business and the passion of his acting.

Recognizing that his fire was attached to his acting career, he made a decision for the first time, and surprisingly he was able to find a connection between a business idea and his acting passion. Sometimes the choice is not between the two things you want most, but rather in creating a third option that you may never have considered before. Often, the choice we make can be a blend of the two things that we want most. Perhaps that is what is meant when people tell you that you can have your cake and eat it too. The challenge that most people experience is that they rarely look for a connection between the things they want.

Exercise - Consider the different things that you want and are splitting your focus and activity. Is there a connection between these things that you might be able to create? Is there a third option you could create that would allow you to make progress toward your goals and dreams?

I wanted to understand change, like really understand it. So, I decided to interview those people who make big shifts or changes for people, and one of the people I decided to interview was a lady who trains suicide hotline workers. If you think about it, people calling a suicide hotline are at their absolute worst despair. They're in the moment of the worst turmoil and the worst challenge that they've ever experienced, and when I asked her about the training they give their operators, she said that we can tell them pretty much anything that they need to hear, except one thing. They can't tell someone, don't kill yourself. I said, "what?" That's like the first thing that I would say, and then she explained that the reason we don't say it is that it takes away choice. - Douglas Vermeeren

It was interesting for me to understand as I spoke with the suicide hotline trainer that shared that. When an individual starts to recognize the power of choice, their power begins to return. In other words, the more choices a person recognizes they have, the more power returns to them.

Exercise - Consider a difficult situation you are facing. Really look carefully at the problem. What are the choices you have in dealing with this? Take time to list all of the possible choices. (Even the ones that you most likely will not employ.) It's also important in this exercise to recognize other sources of help or support that could be available to you. Remember that you don't have to solve all problems by yourself. One of the choices could be to get other people involved to create more solutions.

Because of our wiring, we are not aware of the choices we make, and why we make them, and the things that are driving those choices. Mostly we're not aware that we can make different choices. If the choices that we're making are not serving us, not making us feel good, and make us feel out of alignment, out of integrity or anything else, then we can make different choices, but sometimes we don't know that we can. - Bob Doyle

How to Preselect Clarity

Most people struggle with the concept of clarity. They don't understand what it is, why they need it, or most especially how to find it. The tragedy of that lack of understanding is that clarity is required to experience any form of creation or manifestation. A goal that is specific and clear becomes attainable and near.

Without clarity, you are destined to bumble around from situation to situation without much progress to create the outcomes you desire. Without a target it doesn't matter where you aim or what you do. So how can we build clarity and how does it all fit together?

Our heart is our thinker. Our mind is our creator, and when we can begin to learn how to get clear from our intuitive thought processes or intuitive knowing, then we can begin to bring that awareness up into our mind and begin to create what that will look like. We can begin to create the actions that we need to take, the thoughts we need to hold, and the belief systems that we need to build within ourselves, in order to bring that into our current reality.
- Meagan Fettes

Creation of clarity starts first in our heart. In the other chapters, we often substitute the word heart for intuition, feelings or instinct. Sometimes this creation can be described as getting in touch with our passion and purpose. The most important element to remember here is that our greatest self is found through our heart.

Years ago, as I began my interviews and research of the world's top achievers, I realized quickly that the world in general has a poor definition of success. Most often, success is defined in terms of results, accomplishmeor a specific outcome. While this is an important element of success, it is the weaker part of it. Success must have a sense of connection to your feelings and most especially the things you value.

One of my favorite quotes around this idea comes from Stephen Covey in his book "The 7 Habits of Highly Effective People," he pointed out that, "Many people climb the ladder of success only to find that it's leaning against the wrong wall."

The results we achieve mean nothing unless they are connected to the things we value most. Clarity in your heart must be the foundation of all worthwhile endeavors.

People tend to do what's most important to them. If it's not congruent with their values, they're not going to put the effort into making changes and to move forward. - Jason Parker

We will also find that when we set out to accomplish things that have meaning to us, we will strive harder and get more commitment than we otherwise would. Perhaps that's where the wisdom in Meagan's saying really shines. Once our heart has done the thinking, which is the true evaluation process of what's important to us, then our mind can rise to start putting together the pieces that will allow us to begin the manifestation process.

When a thought is not clear, when it is not specific, when it does not have parameters, when it does not have colors and textures and things that you can clearly see in it, people are limited by that, and what they do is they create a nebulous input. - Denis Waitley

After identifying the feelings of the results you are wishing to create, and you are sure they will bring you more joy and happiness, it is essential to define with clarity our outcome. That's right, feelings of outcome proceed clarity of the aspects of the outcome. A great way to express the direction, commitment and activities is to set and share your intentions.

Intentions rally the forces in your body and mind to go in a particular direction. - Joe Vitale

Intentions can be expressed privately through writings or affirmations, but our intentions should also be shared with others around us. Expressing our intentions is like practicing a sport or learning a musical instrument. The more we do it, the more we develop our abilities and beliefs. As others become aware of our intentions, they can help.

Perhaps another powerful consideration, especially for those involved in relationships, is to recognize that when we share our intentions, that helps others have correct expectations about what we are doing and seeking in our life. Where there are no surprises, there is generally greater peace. Recently at one of my Personal Power Mastery seminars, a newly married couple shared several challenges they were experiencing with being married. Sometimes these new situations had created some arguments that became somewhat heated. As they explored the source of these challenges, it became clear that they hadn't communicated their intentions, which in turn did not give each other a fair expectation of what the other partner desired.

As they developed the skills of better communication, they were able to easier understand each other and develop better expectations of how they could support each other. The funny conclusion of this episode is that they also discovered how similar their intentions were and as a result were able to create even better ways to support each other.

Exercise - Take a moment and consider some of the outcomes you want to create. How are you sharing those intentions with those around you? Make notes about how those around you react as you share these intentions and be especially aware of those who want to help you to achieve those intentions and goals.

We can gain clarity around our thoughts, by noticing the reactions within our physical body. Every single thought will trigger a reaction within our physical body that as soon as we can start to notice how we're reacting based upon that one process of thought, we can begin to notice if that's a thought process that we want to keep, or if we want to cultivate change within that. Our job then is to be aware of the thoughts. - Meagan Fettes

Your physiology affects your emotional mind. So how you actually hold yourself and carry yourself has a big impact on what's actually not only going on in your head, but what you bring into the world. So, let's do a little experiment for right now. As you're sitting in your chair reading this, I want you to just slump down in your chair and think about how you're actually feeling. What are the thoughts that are going in your mind and how is that different? Now stand and take a confident pose, shoulders back, breathing fully in and out. How do you feel in comparison? Recognize how your physiology affects your mind, how it affects your thoughts and how it affects your feelings in general. - Jason Parker

Visualize

Visualization is something you may have heard of before, but most of the time when it is talked about, the conversation shares only a basic view of what it is and how important it could be to manifesting outcomes in your life.

Visualization is not an accidental exercise. Instead, it is a deliberate and focused preview of the reality you are intending to create.

As your thoughts begin to form and strengthen around an idea, your mind starts to visualize what this may look like in reality. This is a crucial step to manifesting what you want. If you can see what you really desire in your mind's eye with clarity, you will begin the creation process. The more power and substance that you add to this visualization, the greater strength it will gain and the faster you will experience it in reality.

Build an image of the good you desire. Internalize it, stand then move into the vibration and attract it. Everything operates on frequencies, and when we're on the frequency of what we don't want, we need to move into the frequency of what we do want. - Bob Proctor

Visualization, for most people, is simply seeing an image of the victory in their mind. Yet there is much more to the creation of your victory than the arrival. It is important to visualize the process and even consider the challenges and how you all overcome them. Often having correct or realistic expectations at the beginning of the process will give you increased power and strength to create the outcome you are seeking.

When you take something that is written--a sentence, a word, a vision board, an image or collage of images, and you close your eyes, you see yourself achieving that goal, that vision, that thing, or becoming that person or overcoming a fear or overcoming low self-esteem. When you start to mentally rehearse that thing, you're actually activating one of the biggest parts of your brain called the occipital lobe, the part of the brain used a lot for visual processing. So, when you deliberately activate that occipital lobe, the visual processing part of your brain, you practice, seeing and feeling yourself, overcoming any obstacles, achieving the goal in the lifestyle and the goodness that comes with achieving your goals, you're training your brain and you're reinforcing new neural patterns. When you do that for 30 days, 60 days, 90 days, 180 days, your brain starts to make everything that you've been visualizing automatic. It starts to force other parts of your brain to think about how can you achieve that. - John Assaraf

Visualization is not an exercise in pretending. In fact, the more realistic you can make your visualizing experience, the more useful it will be to you. In your mind's eye, do all you can to feel the experience in your senses. How does it feel emotionally? How does it feel in a tactile sense? How does it taste? What do you smell? What do you see? What do you hear?

Take time to go deep into the visualization of what you are trying to create. Remember that all things are created spiritually before they are created tangibly and physically in the real world.

Pure visualization is simulation, and simulation is doing what you want to do as if it's the real thing. So, you have to have all the moods and all the mechanisms around you to do it right. What you visualize and internalize will materialize, if you do it right. - Denis Waitley

When done effectively your mind will transfer your created experience into your subconscious mind. As you repeat and practice visualizing, your mind interprets this visualization as a real experience if you have made it real.

If you feel and believe that the experience will be as you create it and add all of the sensory connections, it will be as though it is real. Your brain gives you credit for experiences that you have. Your brain will also give you credit for experiences that you visualize even though you did not participate in the experience.

Visualization is important because it's one of the ways the subconscious mind communicates. It's one way to program the subconscious mind. The subconscious mind is thinking in terms of imagery, the conscious mind is thinking in terms of more of words, but if you want to influence the subconscious mind or change the subconscious mind, you have to have images for that. - Joe Vitale

It is interesting to note that although your brain interprets and is affected by words, those words are actually representations of imagery. By visualizing imagery, your brain more readily accepts what you are creating visually. When you add emotion to the images, they are amplified.

Visualization is a creative process. I have observed several who have taken this idea of creativity in visualization to higher degrees. In addition to conducting a visualizing exercise in their mind alone, they have painted, sketched, written poetry or even written songs to express how they see their future. The energy and power in this creative process has greatly magnified the power of visualizing for them.

Exercise - An interesting note on visualization: Personally, I like the idea of a vision board. Over the years I have observed many different ways people use this tool to manifest new outcomes in their life. Most frequently people construct vision boards by clipping photographs of images that resonate with them or depict items they want to have in their life. I think this is a good beginning.

However, something you may wish to add has been very beneficial for me. My vision boards add two elements that I haven't really seen in the vision boards of other people. I like to include some words. The first set of words I add are emotional words that speak to my reasons why the item on the vision board is important to me and what it really means.

The more important my why, the easier it is to stay focused and make things happen. The more powerful your WHY-power, the more powerful your WILL-power.

The second set of words has to do with clarity. For example, on one of my vision boards I had a picture of a Ferrari. The writing on the vision board reflected with clarity the model, the year and a few other details including the price.

Remember: A goal that is specific and clear becomes attainable and near.

By listing the price, it gave me specific power. The way that this story concluded was, because I had a clear understanding of the specifics of that Ferrari on my vision board, I was able to recognize a really good deal when it appeared as an opportunity in reality.

Vision boards are about more than just clipping pictures. They are about creating it as a tangible possibility in your future. The more you can shape the vision into reality, the more likely it is that it will arrive.

When you start to see yourself achieving those goals, becoming that person who can achieve her goals or his goals, then you're actually also going to activate a part of the brain called the nucleus accumbens and insula, which releases dopamine, that feel good neurochemical that then your brain gets addicted to, so that it starts to cause that which you've been visualizing to actually happen in your life because it's going to help you take action towards it. - John Assaraf

A powerful support to add to your visualization is to journal about your experience and capture your feelings about it. Record it as though it was a real experience and solidify the power of it in your mind.

Your Brain Doesn't Get Started with Everything
Thoughts become things when you act upon them over time, with emotion and repetition. - Denis Waitley

Ripple effect
Like a pebble being dropped into a pond, your thoughts and actions create ripples in your life. As these ripples are created and proceed outward, they connect with affect, and influence those around you.

Sometimes, these ripples are well received. Other times, they can create abrasive or non-supporting responses. Sometimes, those connections can create secondary ripples, and sometimes those connections can create so much energy that it's almost like you have a tsunami on your hands.

The ripple effect is one way to clearly see the steps of how your thoughts will become things.

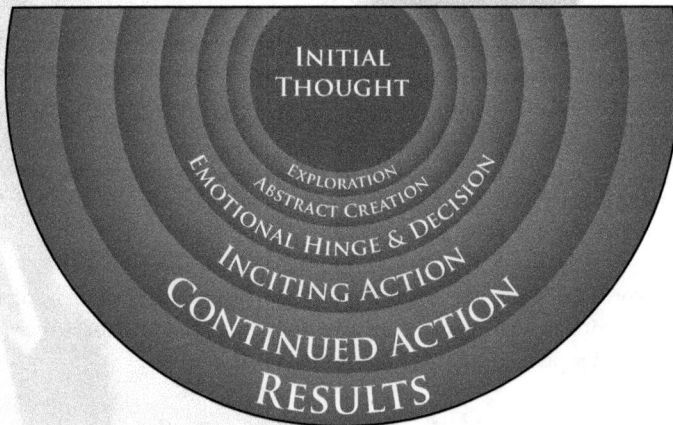

Not all ripples are strong enough to carry a thought into reality. Only those with emotion and connection to our highest values can turn a ripple into a wave.

Habit
Habits are the result of attempting activities and finding that it gave you enough value to repeat it again. Some habits can be extremely useful and beneficial, while others may have become redundant and stale. What served you yesterday may be holding you back today.

When you wake up in the morning, chances are that you automatically do certain things, whether it's get coffee, brush your teeth, stretch, do a gratitude exercise, etc. The more you do that, the more your brain says, I'm just going to make this automatic. - Travis Fox

Habits are your brain's way of streamlining things in your life. By doing so, it preserves energy and time in evaluating.

From a neuroscience point of view, habits are created whenever we repeat. It's a thought pattern, an emotional pattern or behavioral pattern, either on their own, or as an integrated set of anything that we repeat, because the brain is always looking to conserve energy. Anytime we put exerted force or anytime something happens repetitively, automatically our brain says, "You know what, let me just make this thing that you consciously do automatic." So for every habit, there's always a trigger. Something that triggers that habit loop, we call it. - John Assaraf

We frequently hear the idea that it takes 30 days to construct a new habit. The truth is that habit is only partially created by repetition. The other part of habit is created by conviction. The decision to create a new habit and the conviction to begin it are the most powerful when you can clearly see the connection between a new habit and an outcome that is extremely valuable to you.

I have observed people who have been able to create a new habit in hours because it was extremely important to them, and I have also seen people who've been struggling to create a new habit for themselves for years.

Habits can be created by default or on purpose, but whether we are aware or not, habits are always being created and nurtured.

To become an Olympic medalist, I had to develop the habits that Olympic medalists would have. What does that look like? The habits of an Olympic medalist aren't sleeping in or skipping workouts. The habit of an Olympic medalist is waking up every single day with the intention of being better that day than they were the day before, and then following through on all of those things. - Jason Parker

Exercise - Consider some of the habits that you currently have in your life. Can you identify which ones serve you best and perhaps more importantly what are the outcomes and consequences being created by these habits? Try and identify which ones are no longer serving you. Again, they were not necessarily wrong when you developed them, but times and situations have changed since then. It's okay to start replacing them with new habits that lead to a better version of you.

Exercise - Habits are like markers or guideposts that can help you to achieve the outcomes you want in your life. Outcomes are most often the result of the things that we habitually do. So, if you want to experience better outcomes it stands to reason that one of the most important things you can do is to develop better habits.

Take a careful look at people who have achieved the same outcomes that you would like to create. Can you identify what habits they have that have specifically helped to create the outcomes that you are now desiring? How can you duplicate and even improve those same habits in your life? How often are those habits turning into action in their life?

Measurement

Measurement is something that is not often discussed in the journey of turning thoughts into things. Measurement is observing the results or outcomes of certain thoughts and activities and then fine-tuning those thoughts and activities to generate outcomes that are closer to what is desired.

Generally speaking, outcomes do not arrive perfect or fully finished. Measurement is like fine-tuning a radio receiver to bring the results we have created to more closely resemble the outcomes we desire.

There is great freedom in having correct expectations about how our outcomes will arrive. If we expect that things will arrive close but not perfect, we experience less pressure to get things perfect. It may be worth pointing out that perfection doesn't exist anyway. Make progress towards your goal, not perfection.

The only way we can generate success is to recognize that it is a function of progression.

That raises the question as to how progress can be created without measurement. It can't. In order to make progress, you need to understand where you are and where the activities you are engaging in are taking you. Are they bringing you closer to the outcomes you desire or creating a larger gap between you and what you want?

Exercise - In order for measurement to be effective, you need to measure frequently and have some clarity around what you will measure. Measurement typically involves some form of record keeping. A journal is generally the most accepted way to measure progress in getting to your goals. Start by outlining the outcome you are looking to create. Clarity of purpose and outcome are at the beginning success. Next outline the thinking and activities that you are engaged in that are directly connected to creating the desired outcome. Next, identify how these activities and thinking have helped you move towards the goal.

I find it valuable to give a rating as to how effective the activities have been. This is now a good time to reflect and explore if there is in fact a better way to approach creating the desired outcome. Through consistent measurement and questions, you will be pleased to see progress come quickly and steadily.

Measurement with a Mentor

It has been said that if you are within the frame, you can't see the picture. Sometimes we are far too close to our lives to often recognize what needs to be done within them. Our biases and limited perspectives in the moment often keep us from seeing things how they really are or even worse - what they could be.

Having an accountability partner, coach or mentor helps us to measure our progress and can be a very helpful tool. It has been said that the most valuable thing a mentor can help us see are things about ourselves that we didn't know before that moment.

Exercise - Set out on a mission to find mentors to support you in your journey to create the outcomes you desire in your life. Consider finding a mentor for the specific 5 pillar areas of your life. It is important to remember that not all mentors are able to help you in each area of your life.

Once you have this mentor, consider how often you will connect with and learn from them. Also think carefully about how you will record, keep and implement the wisdom they give to you.

From my experience, it's also important to meet regularly and report back to your mentor. It should not be a one-time experience, but rather an ongoing relationship where that mentor can help you, see the results, help you make adjustments and move forward.

Questions - How Do thoughts become things?
How are you using your focus to create the outcomes you desire?
Is there a third option you could select that might allow you to experience two things you desire?
How important are intentions?
Why should you share these intentions with others?
How does having correct expectations create better harmony in relationships?
What can we learn from the example of the newlyweds?
How can you use visualization to manifest your desired outcomes?
What are some common mistakes most people make with visualization?
How can you use a vision board to facilitate manifesting the outcomes you desire?
What should be included on your vision board?
What does your brain need to understand in order to be convinced to take action?
Describe the ripple effect.
How did your habits start?
What habits have you developed that are no longer serving you?
What habits are serving you best right now?
What habits could you develop that would help you to create the outcomes you desire?
Who is demonstrating habits connected to outcomes you want to manifest?
How can you develop the same habits?
How are you measuring the results of your thoughts?
What role does measurement have in turning your thoughts into things?
What is the power of measurement?
How does measurement give us freedom?
What have you chosen to measure?
How can you use the support of a mentor or accountability partner in measurement?

HOW
THOUGHTS
BECOME THINGS™

Emotions are the big amplifier and magnifier. -Dr. Marina Bruni

If you just have a random thought, it will not be so impactful, but if you have a thought with an intention and energy behind it, that is something. A strength, a passion, a joyous gratitude thought really has an effect of in your life. - Marie Diamond

By now, you've experienced millions of thoughts in your life. As you've felt and observed these thoughts, it has been evident that not all thoughts have equal power. Not all the thoughts you have will manifest new realities or experiences for you. In fact, the majority of the thoughts you have don't really create much individually.

So, what is it about certain thoughts that give them the ability to manifest new outcomes in your life? What is it about some thoughts that change your direction or even your beliefs? What makes some thoughts powerful? And what makes other thoughts more or less inert?

If you have a thought about something you would like to have, do or be, you've got to fuel it with fire. And what's the fire? The fire is emotion. - Joe Vitale

Emotion is a secret fuel to igniting thought into reality. Thoughts without emotion tend to disappear or dissipate quickly, but when a thought has a powerful emotion attached to it, magical things happen.

American psychologist William James said that our emotions, which are also a component of our thoughts, follow motion. So, here's an idea. When you want to interrupt a negative thought or a pattern, it's not enough to just say stop. The reality is, it's time to get in motion by doing something different. - Jason Parker

The reason why is that thoughts in and of themselves have very little power or influence. As pointed out earlier, most thoughts occur as a reaction to an external stimulus.

However, most of the stimuli we encounter daily tend to produce aneutral responses. In other words, the majority of the stimuli we encounter in our daily routines don't really evoke any kind of significant thought responses.

Yet when one stimulus provokes a strong emotion, it causes us to stop and analyze it. This thought then gains power, and if the emotion is strong enough, it calls forth action. If the thought continues down the same course of strong emotion, the actions become stronger.

While this information about emotion can be used to our advantage with positive situations, it is important to point out that negative emotions can enhance negative situations. As an example of this, think about the last time you were involved in a negative situation like an argument. The more your negative emotions became involved in the situation, your feelings of frustration rose.

Most likely, as your emotions escalated you either did or said some things that were not productive or supportive in the situation.

We need to be very careful to recognize what kinds of emotions are propelling us to action. The law of attraction attracts the things we feel most strongly about whether they are the things we love or the things we hate.

The more you can feel love for it, the more you'll attract it. The rule of thumb in neuro-psychology is that you attract what you love, what you hate and what you fear. Most people are focused on what they hate and what they fear. You want to focus on what you love. - Joe Vitale

Naturally, the deeper connection to emotions we can find between our thoughts and the things we want, the easier it will be to take action creating the outcomes we want. As humans, we generally only take action on things that have emotional meaning to us. The more emotional meaning we can establish for a thing, the more motivated we are to take action and continue acting.

Emotion is not only the glue, but it is the driving force that cements thoughts. You know what they always say, you won't remember what I say. You won't remember what you've learned, but you will remember what you felt about the experience that we had that day. Your feelings are the things that linger, not the learning lessons themselves. - Denis Waitley

It is interesting to observe that the words emotion and motion actually come from the same root word, but the connection isn't just with the etymology of the words. Emotions put us into motion, and as we are involved in motion or taking action, our emotions around a certain thing solidify and become more entrenched.

As we make a conscious effort to notice and amplify our emotions around the things that we want, we gain more power to stay focused, make sacrifices where necessary, act and keep working through minor setbacks as they appear.

Emotion plus motion equals manifestation of the reality that you want. - Joe Vitale

Most people only get moving or into motion as they feel like it. The key word is feel. When you feel something about the thoughts you are having, you act on them.

When we attach our emotion to that particular thought, we amplify the effect of the energy that is being generated by the thought. - Marina Bruni

Most people resist getting their emotions involved in their manifesting processes. They assume that goal setting or similar activities are to be governed by our logical mind. While we often use our logical mind to think about the futures we wish to manifest, it is our emotional mind that needs to become involved in order to create activity in the present.

Emotion is absolutely essential. Without emotion, your thoughts become just an intellectual game you're playing with yourself, and unfortunately that's what a lot of people do. They're so intellectual, they're so brainy, that they don't let themselves get emotionally involved. - Bob Proctor

Naturally, as we pursue our goals, we will encounter difficulties that may require perseverance or change. If we approach solely from a logical point of view, we will find great difficulty to find the power we need to see a thing through.

Understanding who we are at an emotional level gives us a sense of purpose and a sense of being. When we are only focused on the logical component, it's easy to just focus on what we are doing.

When we focus exclusively on the logical component of taking action, we lose a portion of our true power. We must have a purpose for doing so. We are human beings after all, not human doings.

We've got to turn our ideas over to the emotional mind, and the emotional mind is the spiritual essence of who we are as universal intelligence. So, you're turning the idea of universal intelligence, it's like giving it to God, let go, let God, then it'll move into form, and without the emotion behind the idea, filled by natural death, ideas are still-born and that's unfortunately where most of them go. - Bob Proctor

Emotions shape our perspective and interpretations of reality. We only attach meaning to the things we have feelings about. If we don't care about a thing, it goes unnoticed, and it's almost like it doesn't exist.

The more we care about something, the more important it is to us. In real life, we protect the things we care most about. We do the same thing with our thoughts.

Emotions are the most powerful thing when we have a thought. That's when we deem it to be real. - Meagan Fettes

When we truly care about a thought, we hold it carefully in a protected way. We focus on it differently. We guard it and defend it. We search for ways to give that thought more power and strength.

The good news is that we can choose what thoughts we will choose to get emotionally charged. Naturally, we don't get to choose the initial response, but we can choose the fire that we will light under it.

This really is the secret on how to direct your thoughts. It is holding the emotional state, and then letting that emotion percolate up into the subconscious. So, once it gets to the subconscious, it's going to then pull from all of your prior experiences where you have felt that feeling before. It's going to wrap around it just like a bubble, and it's going to help that emotion then get strengthened at the neurological level. You start getting a habit, and then it's going to direct your conscious mind to be on guard in a positive way, looking around your environment. - Travis Fox

Exercise - Think about some of the things that you really want to manifest in your life. What kinds of emotions do you have attached to these things? Why do you have these emotions about these things? What can you do to enhance these emotions to make them more powerful around these thoughts?

Some people have suggested that at times they have had a hard time understanding what thoughts excite them and what thoughts frighten them. Sometimes when we undertake to do something new, we can experience both.

Exercise - What similarities have you experienced between emotions that you have experienced? Think about why you may have labelled an excitement in the past as a fear? Or a thrilling excitement as nervousness? Take a moment and journal about how some of these experiences, which started out as frightening, may have been exhilarating for you and how the end result was a blessing instead of a detriment.

Our Highest Values Dictate Our Priorities

Our emotions generally follow our values. We have good emotions when we experience something that supports our values and beliefs, and we experience challenging emotions when we encounter things that conflict with our values and beliefs.

In our day-to-day life, we gravitate towards activities that support our highest values and avoid or procrastinate things which we feel are not connected to those values. This is why when outside forces assign us a goal or a quota that doesn't resonate with our true values, we resist. A wise leader understands that, to get others to support their vision, they must share the vision in a way that all involved can personally adopt that same vision as their own in an authentic way.

This doesn't just apply to an outside manager. We are all managers of our own behavior. Oftentimes, we declare a goal or an outcome that we desire. We know that we want it logically, but because it's not truly in alignment with our highest values, we procrastinate or avoid doing anything.

Exercise - Habits and activities in our lives generally began because, at one point in time, we felt they would bring us the things we valued most in life. Finding out redundant or irrelevant activities that no longer serve us can be a valuable exercise. However, often they are difficult to pinpoint. Rather than try and identify the weeds, so to speak, most people have found more value to crowd out the weeds by filling their life with activities and new habits that serve them better. Consider your current highest values. What are some habits that would serve you better?

How you show up determines what shows up for you. The universe is an echo chamber.

The unified energy field responds to us and sends back to us an equal amount of energy or the corresponding frequency vibration or frequency that we have sent out. - Dr. Marina Bruni

Influence

Everything that we surround ourselves with has an influence and impact on our thoughts. Our thoughts dictate and direct our beliefs about everything we believe is possible. The environment that we create or allow around us determines what feelings, emotions and beliefs will grow within us, and then what's within us returns back to us to create more of what's around us.

Influence really does change our lives because we have success and failure by association. We hang around people who are successful, and they help us be more successful. We hang around with people who know more, do more, feel more, love more, are more optimistic, and it rubs off on us. Don't hang around with people who have similar problems. For example, if you were recently fired, don't hang around with people who are recently fired because your pity party is just group griping or commiserating. Hang around with people well employed, recently employed, or have become entrepreneurs. So, my best advice is, increase your thinking, increase your network. - Denis Waitley

Exercise - Take an inventory of some of the influences in your life. As thoughts are created through stimulus, it stands to reason that they rise or fall to the kinds of influences in your life. Influences are found in environment, activities and associations. Make a list of things you are deliberately allowing to influence you in these areas of your life.

Consideration - What influences are coming into your life without deliberate creation and how are they affecting you?

Decision
Once we make a decision, and realize that action is required, many people start experiencing fear and doubt. These emotions can paralyze us and stop powerful thoughts from proceeding toward a tangible creation.

Too often, people make decisions based on where they are rather than where they want to go. They don't understand how decisions really are the pathway to a new future and have very little to do with the here and now. While you may see scarcity, lack and challenge in the present, the best decisions operate based on a positive, hopeful and optimistic outlook.

The word "optimistic" shares the same root as the word "optimize." "Optimize" doesn't mean "perfection required." Instead, to optimize means to take any situation and improve it for the greatest good. When you make a decision, you need to look for how you can optimize whatever you are currently experiencing.

When you know in your mind that you want to do this, you need to make a decision. Decision has actually been very misunderstood. See, most people make a decision based on their current circumstances when an opportunity comes, and they say things like, I don't have enough time, or I don't have enough money. I don't know enough, I'm not skilled enough. What these people fail to understand is that decisions have very little to do with the present, you're already here. Decisions affect the future. So, if you want more time, more money, more knowledge, more skills, more opportunity, you need to start by making a new decision. - Douglas Vermeeren

It doesn't happen by accident. It happens because you've decided. Then you've got to prepare yourself for it to happen. - Bob Proctor

Decisions are never a decision, until action is attached. - Douglas Vermeeren

Deliberate action
If you were to engage in a conversation around achievement, goal-setting or any other conversation around the concept of manifesting your desires, it won't take you long to hear someone proclaim that you need to take massive action.

When I first heard this idea of massive action, I was also sucked into believing that was the answer. After all. massive action should produce massive results right?

In theory, it sounds correct.

It was a short time into my personal interviews with more than 400 of the world's top achievers that I noticed that the idea of massive action was not practiced by these elite achievers. In fact, it was clear that most of these high-level achievers had a much different approach to action. They did not take massive action. In fact, they often said no to activities more often than they said yes. Their goal wasn't to find a way to do more or get more done.

At first, I was in disbelief and was quite confused. While everyone was proclaiming massive action as the solutions to all the problems, these multi-millionaires and billionaires were doing the opposite. I decided to investigate further. I decided to ask one of these achievers if he would allow me to shadow him for the day. He agreed. We started early at a breakfast meeting. I noticed that he very carefully reviewed a series of specific objectives.

As we sat at breakfast, his assistant brought by several papers and invitations for phone calls or meetings that day. Quickly he sorted through the new items and eliminated almost everything that had arrived. Immediately he could tell I had a question, and he told me to go ahead and ask it. "Why had he eliminated some of those things, and how did he decide which ones to keep? Wasn't he worried he might be removing some important items that might be worth pursuing to generate more money?

Paraphrasing he said, "The goal is not to be busy, but productive." As I thought about that answer then and many times since, I have come to the conclusion why most people struggle to get ahead in life, business, relationships or whatever else they are trying to achieve. Most people don't have a boundary between what actions are really contributing to the outcomes they desire to create.

They are content taking action just to be busy. When true progress comes from selecting the right things to get busy with so that you are creating progress.

Exercise - Consider some of the things you are trying to create right now. Identify what activities in your day are actually contributing to that outcome and drawing you closer to what you want. A useful exercise might be to record your activities throughout the day for a complete week. Take a careful look at why you chose to spend your time and effort with these specific activities and the rewards they created for you in the end.

In the same way, identify things you are doing that are just keeping you busy and not contributing to that outcome. How can you build better boundaries around your time and your efforts so they can be directed to more effectiveness?

I learned that day and many times since that deliberate action is almost more valuable than busy action, but it is easier to create busy action than deliberate action because busy action doesn't require as much careful thinking or planning.

If you want to create better outcomes in your life spend more time planning your actions.

Questions - The fuel and the hinge

What role does emotion play in achieving your desires?

How are emotion and motion related?

How can you increase your feelings around the important thoughts you have?

Why do some of your thoughts provoke more emotion than others?

What kinds of thoughts do you get most emotional about?

How can we increase emotion around our thoughts?

How does emotion help us stay focused in difficult times?

Why is emotion more important than the logical brain?

Why are negative and positive emotions sometimes similar?

Why is massive action not the goal?

Why do most people procrastinate?

What should a manager or leader do to help others get on board with their vision?

How can you determine your highest values?

What is your strongest why?

How will you keep your why at the top of your thoughts each day?

Do you have a clear understanding of your highest values?

Are your immediate activities in line with your highest values?

Why is massive action not the right answer?

What's the difference between massive busy actions and deliberate action?

How can you ensure your actions are more deliberate?

HOW THOUGHTS BECOME THINGS™

TARGETING YOUR FUTURE AND SEEING POSSIBILITY

5 Ways Your Brain Learns

Research has shown that our mind processes and sorts information in specific ways. In the live trainings, we talk about this as the 5 ways your brain learns. There are many applications when you understand this principle, including everything from sales and persuasion to staying focused with goals that matter most.

The five ways that your brain learns and processes information are as follows:

Fact
Experience
Social
Spatial
Intuition

Let me explain each:

Fact - When our mind recognizes something as fact or something that we believe to be factually true, we work with that information in a particular way, and we store it separately. As an example, if you received 2+2 =4 as a fact, you would store it and recall it in a unique way compared with other information you would learn.

However, it is important to point out that information that we receive as fact does not necessarily mean it is true. Think about this, have you ever been part of a discussion where the other person had a different set of facts than you? No doubt you were convinced that you were right and they were mistaken, and they felt the same way about you. Is it possible that both of you could have been correct? Is it reasonable that two sets of facts could be true? Sometimes.

Experience - There are certain things that you can only learn from experience. This kind of learning incorporates muscle memory. Think of it this way, there are certain things that you can only learn from experience. For example, you can't learn how to play a guitar, ride a bike or do Jiu jitsu through reading a book. The only way you'll learn those activities is through active participation.

Quick note: Sir Isaac Newton is credited with identifying our five senses. Touch, taste, smell, sight and hearing. However, he missed one. Let me be the first to declare that one of your most important senses is balance. Without it, you wouldn't even be able to sit down and read this book.

Social - Social learning often happens without our awareness. Much of social learning is what makes up our values, expectations and belief programming. These are the things that we learn through associations with our family, communities, church groups, peers and others that we spend time with. The values and perceptions of those we spend time with become our own.

Spacial - This is a unique form of learning in that we are continually encountering this one. Spatial learning has to do with how we orient things in regards to one another. Deep perception can be considered part of this. You won't cross the street if you judge the approaching car is moving at a speed that would arrive where you intend to walk precisely at the same time as you.

There are other expressions of spatial learning as well. Every time you hang a picture, play Tetris, build a jigsaw puzzle or put a glass down on a table you are experiencing a form of spatial reasoning. Indeed, it is apparent in almost every way that we interact with our environment.

It might be interesting to point out that spatial reasoning is one of the challenges that people experience when trying to manifest things into their life. We often put the things that we want in a physical realm far away from us and because we believe they are so far away, we prevent them from coming into existence in our immediate environment.

You can pick up the thought of somebody on the other side of the world because there is no other side. That's an illusion. There's no space. That's why when you take a picture of somebody and hit send, they get the image you send simultaneously. - Bob Proctor

There is no other side of the world. Everything is connected. Yet our spatial learning puts things so far away from us.

Intuition - Intuition is perhaps the most powerful way that our mind learns. Sometimes people call this kind of learning our gut-instinct. Most of the time this learning appears in the form of feelings rather than information that is conveyed.

Most of the time, when people speak of this kind of learning, they point to the negative side of intuition. It is true that it is our intuition that warns us that there may be danger or that a person is not telling us the truth. However, our intuition is also the source of our inspiration and most powerful thoughts.

Generally, when you have an idea about a goal you would like to achieve or an accomplishment you would like to pursue, it originates in your intuition. You get a feeling that you could be successful with this new idea.

Most people don't give their intuition enough credit or power. Intuition grows with the use of imagination and creativity, both of which we will talk about later in the book.

If we understand these 5 ways our mind processes information, we can tap into a greater power to manifest the realities we seek after in our lives. Let me illustrate with an example:

As I've stated above, all of the most powerful ideas first arrive in our intuition.

When President Kennedy asked Dr. Wernher von Braun what would it take to build a rocket that would carry man to the moon and bring him back safely, Wernher von Braun answered five words: The will to do it. The will is mental faculties like perception or intuition. It's what gives you the ability to focus, and when you focus, you take this beautiful power that flows in, and you narrow it. When you focus, you send that intention out of your mind, and you increase the amplitude of vibration. Your thought becomes many times more powerful. Now if your thoughts are just idle thoughts, there's no power to them, but when you concentrate, concentration increases amplitude of vibration. There's more power to your thoughts, I think. Emerson quoted it very well. He said, the only thing that grows is the thing you give energy to. How does this happen? It happened because they built the idea in my mind, and I stayed with it. I didn't let anything sidetrack me. - Bob Proctor

Your willingness factor appears in everything you do. It is dangerous to think that your willingness doesn't count, and it's also dangerous to assume that you are not being observed or considered for bigger things when you are involved in things you think don't matter.

Support

Our thoughts and feelings are influenced by those we hold in high regard. We will rise to the standards or expectations of those we value, and we will allow those expectations to contribute to the expectations we have in ourselves.

Teamwork makes the dream work, but do you have the right team and are they aware of the dream? It's nice to have support and a team to help you, but most people have a dysfunctional team. It's not necessarily the team's fault but rather the leader behind the team.

Have you clearly helped your team to see what they're trying to create, or have you left that to chance? Many people in fact feel that if they revealed their true motives to the team, the people involved may not be willing to help. Quite the opposite is actually true.

Most people think that change needs to be hard, but the reason why it's hard for them is because they choose to believe that it needs to be hard. - Jason Parker

Your thoughts manifest themselves faster and easier if they are connected to other people. The great things in life, business relationships, know-how, and even abundance have always been a result of collaboration with others. If you'll look at even getting to the moon or climbing Mount Everest or winning gold medals at the Olympics or even creating multinational billion-dollar brands, they're always the work of a team. - Douglas Vermeeren

Questions - Targeting your future and seeing possibility
How can understanding the 5 ways your brain learns help you manifest what you want in life?
How would you describe factual learning and how is it valuable to you?
Is it possible to have different facts than others?
Is it possible to believe "facts" that are not based on truth or reality?
How would you describe experiential learning and how is it valuable to you?
What things have you learned through experience in the past?
How would you describe social learning and how is it valuable to you?
How would you describe spatial learning and how is it valuable to you?
How would you describe intuitive learning and how is it valuable to you?
Why is intuitive learning so important?
Which area do our greatest regrets come from?
How can you use the 5 ways your mind learns to create more power to manifest what you want?
When was the last time you spent time to construct your future?
What is the willingness factor?
How willing are you?

HOW
THOUGHTS
BECOME THINGS™

OVERCOMING NEGATIVE THOUGHTS

One way to beat these negative emotions is to get clarity about those thoughts and find the opposite emotions of those thoughts.

I have long observed that the two most powerful influencing factors that hold most people back from success are either their peers or their fears. We have chatted above about the influence of our peers and networks. We will now talk about fear, where it comes from and the influence it has on you.

To begin this discussion, it is important to point out that all negative feelings have some common connections with positive feelings.

Nervousness, fear and hesitation--these are all closely related to excitement, power and enthusiasm. At any given time, we all have these positive, expansive emotions inside us waiting to be released at our command, and even though we may feel fear, doubt or hesitation, we need not fear.

If you listen carefully to the whisperings in your heart, you will already know that any time we have authentic thoughts, the powerful and empowering emotions will always be present. Therefore, the emotions you attach to your thoughts are always more of a choice than you may have realized.

If you're unhappy, if you're dissatisfied, if there is more, if there's something you would like to have, do or be, and you've been frustrated, you are reaching, you are stretching, but it's not happening. It may be time to look at your thoughts because your thoughts are creating your reality. Become aware of your thoughts, choose different thoughts which are going to lead to different actions, and keep elevating your thinking. - Joe Vitale

Fear is very real. So don't ever tell a child, there's nothing to be afraid about, don't be frightened. It's real to the person experiencing it because it's almost an automatic reaction of survival. As we've evolved, fear has kept us alive. When we go out to get something to eat, maybe something will eat us instead. So, we have developed over the millennia, a fight or flight experience using fear as a way to survive or stay alive. - Denis Waitley

The cause of fear is really ignorance. - Bob Proctor

We are influenced by our fears or our peers. - Douglas Vermeeren

Actions That Follow Fear Are What's Most Important
Fear itself never creates results or outcomes. It is important to remember that whatever follows your feelings of fear will make all the difference. The popular idea of "feel the fear and do it anyways" is based in a powerful truth that, as we determine to take action through our fear, we will create a momentum that will help us move beyond fear.

Some people think that to make the Law of Attraction work, to be able to create a life you love, you can never have a negative thought--that is just not true. There's a whole spectrum of emotions that we as human beings are meant to feel. It's about how long are we going to dwell in that negative thought before we change it into something positive that's going to surface. - Bob Doyle

You're designed to have negative thoughts, self-defeating feelings, fears, anxieties, the second you set goals that aren't yours to get you to set more profound goals that are. - Dr. John Demartini

When I went to the start line at the Olympics, I actually had a moment of fear. And this wasn't a fear that was obviously threatening my life. It wasn't a survival fear. It was a fear of ego. What do I mean by that? The fear that I experienced was the fear of what happens if I slip? What happens if I fall? What happens if I'm not strong enough or I'm not good enough today? What would happen? I might let my team down, I might let my family down, I might even let my country down. These are all fears of ego. How I shifted from that was I shifted my mind. I shifted from thinking what if - negative. What if - worst case scenario. Obviously falling, tripping, all those things were worst case scenarios. And I shifted my perspective, to what I refer to as What if - positive. What if - best case scenario. I shifted from fear to asking myself, what if everything happens exactly the way it's meant to happen? - Jason Parker

Toxic People

This is a touchy topic and one that is talked about a lot in personal development circles. While I underline the importance of escaping abuse, we must recognize that we often mislabel difficult conversations or challenging learning moments as toxic or negative.

When it comes to toxic people, I really think that most of the gurus have it wrong. They teach to disconnect and separate yourself from toxic or negative people. And while I do advocate the idea of separating yourself from abusive people, the encouragement that they're giving is that if you feel something or someone makes you feel bad, you should avoid it, or separate that person from your life. Well, the truth is that all people who function at high levels are problem solvers. They don't run from toxic people or people that make them feel bad. They just learn to manage those people better. - Douglas Vermeeren

When you are in a moment where the teaching and the teacher feel uncomfortable, pause for a moment and consider--is this something I actually need to hear? Am I being taught here? If you are being honest with yourself and recognize that there is value, then choose to focus on the outcome. Try and see the love and concern that a bad communicator has for you even though they may not be sensitive in the moment.

Oftentimes, you'll find a negative feeling in a conversation can be improved by simply validating the lesson being shared with you. Showing you are open to trying to see and understand often makes the messenger more kind, sensitive and gentle.

On several occasions, I have been on the receiving end of a valuable set of lessons that was presented to me in an uncomfortable way. On more than one occasion, as the 'toxic teacher' saw that I was invested and willing to listen, their tone softened, and they reframed their lesson with an apology. Then they actually made a more careful effort to not only teach me something I needed to hear but to make sure I was okay at the end.

When we receive like we truly care, these kinds of discussions can actually bind us together rather than draw us apart.

When you're surrounded with people that are positive thinkers, it's easier for you to have more positive thoughts. - Marie Diamond

We're all one soul. So, when we begin to think that we need to cut people out of our lives or we begin to think about toxicity within relationships and dismissing people, we're actually hurting ourselves as well as them. Instead, what would be beneficial is leaning into those relationships, gaining an understanding and different points of view, allowing yourself to let go of the current thought processes that are holding you in that space of that judgment, and allowing yourself to really hear and listen where that person is, to create a solution moving forward. When people show up in our lives, it's not necessarily about them. What is the story that you have about them based on your past experiences? Is there something that they do that triggers a thought process that shifts the way you see them? Notice, and shift your way of thought, because the only thing that you actually have control over, is you, your stories, your ideas, your thoughts, so that you can actually begin to see people and allow them to change and see who they're meant to be. - Meagan Fettes

Scarcity thinking

Scarcity thinking is any form of thinking small or with contraction. Some examples of thinking small include jealousy, comparison, contraction, criticism, doubt, demising, fear, denial or excuse.

Any time we share an excuse we are in the process of creating a limitation. No one ever creates an excuse except for circumstances they could actually do something about.

By excusing ourselves from an opportunity, we are placing a limitation on our future.

It might be interesting to observe that, for most people, when we are invited to participate in an opportunity, the first thought we generally have is to make an excuse so we don't have to participate. Have you ever thought about why that is our first instinct? Some may say that it is a protection mechanism that is designed to keep us safe or to prevent us from danger.

While that may be true, I believe that the real reason is a form of laziness, but wait, let's not be hard on ourselves. One of the primary objectives of the human brain is to look for ways to preserve energy. By simply making an excuse, we are conserving ourselves for those moments of danger when we may really need to act.

However, proactivity is a common attribute of high level manifesters. If we want to expand what we have in life, we must be by expanding who we are which also means we need to expand what we are willing to do.

Exercise - What excuses do we find ourselves repeating to escape participation in an opportunity? What would happen if we said yes instead?

Exercise - We've all heard about affirmations, but in case you're new to the idea, it's essentially planting the seeds in your mind for how you want the future to be by repeating self-affirming thoughts or ideas aloud to yourself. Many people swear by affirmations and have found great results in doing these. I am a fan of affirmations, but I want to invite you to push these affirmations even a step further by attaching a specific action you will do to the affirmation. In my seminars we call these Affirm-actions. Make a list right now of the results you would like to create through affirmations and then attach an affirmation to each one.

Questions - Overcoming negative thoughts
What is the purpose of our feelings?
How do emotions and feelings help us manifest the outcomes we desire?
How are positive and negative feelings similar?
How have your negative thoughts been a source of power?
What is fear?
How does surrounding yourself with positive people help you create positive outcomes?
How is the universe like an echo chamber?
What is scarcity thinking?
How can an affirm-action help you create the results you want in your life?

HOW
THOUGHTS
BECOME THINGS™

You have now been introduced to the beginning of how your thoughts become things. What will you do with what you have learned? What will you create? What will you imagine into reality? What will you bring into your life? The power is yours. You've had it all along. What will you do next?

What's next? Who is it that you really want to become? What thoughts, ideas or beliefs do you need to create about yourself, about the world around you, so that you can begin to show up as your best self, so that you can tap into that potential that resides within you and live the life that you're meant to live? - Meagan Fettes

Most people never realize the amazing potential that is within them and the opportunities that surround them daily. Instead of intentionally creating the life they want by design, they often wait until something amazing arrives for them. The truth is that rarely do amazing possibilities arrive on their own. They are always created with intention.

Exercise - Take some time right now and think about how you would prefer your life to be. Consider all of the significant areas of your life. How do you want to feel about yourself? How do you want to feel about your spirituality? How do you want to feel about your health? How do you want to feel about your relationships? How do you want to feel about your abundance? Once you have identified how you want to feel about these areas of your life, consider what would have to happen in order for these feelings to be created. This is actually a very good series of questions to revisit often.

Once you have determined what needs to happen, work backwards and consider the thinking that you will have to habitually incorporate to start drawing these things into your life. Consider the influences and support mechanisms that you will need to establish in order to facilitate these changes. Consider what old thinking, habits, relationships and influences around you that you may need to shift, dissolve or remove from your life in order to support where you want to go now.

When you know how this looks with clarity, get started and get committed on creating it. Return often to the different sections in this book that will support you with manifesting these things in reality. Now that you know how to do it - it's time to get started.

Give yourself permission to be you. The most magnificent you'll ever be, achieved. No fantasy can ever give you what you can offer. - Dr. John Demartini

Authenticity and choosing to be you, the real you, is one of the greatest senses of validation you will ever receive. The good news is that you are good enough, and the choices you want to make for you are correct.

In addition, the more authentic your choices are to your truest self, the more power you will have in creating the outcomes you desire. When you truly recognize the value in what you want to create for yourself, you will have power, validation, happiness and fulfillment. Too often, people lose all of those things when they try to create outcomes which are suggested or influenced by outside sources.

Clarity

In my Personal Power Mastery seminars, there is a saying that I often share:

A goal that is specific and clear, becomes attainable and near.

When I meet with someone who struggles to manifest new outcomes in their life, the most common challenge is clarity. Most people do not know what they really want. As a result, they are not able to receive it when it appears. Because they have never invested the effort to get clear about what they want, they live a life of reaction rather than creation. They accept what comes because they can't call out to and create what they want.

It has been startling for me to see that everything you could possibly want is within reach, but until you determine with clarity what you want, you cannot receive what you want or draw boundaries around yourself to protect yourself from what you don't want.

Exercise - Take some time each week to gain more insight and clarity of what you truly want, why you want it and the outcomes that achieving this thing will create for you in the future. The more we can establish clarity around what we want, the more we will recognize how to create it in our day to day lives.

Decisions & Absolutes

Most people don't understand that decisions are one of our greatest sources of power. Once we recognize we have choices as to how we want our life to be, we can make decisions to support those desires.

However, even when people say that they are making a decision, they are not able to create results. The reason is simply they haven't understood what decisions are.

A decision is much more than a declaration. In fact, decisions don't truly exist until there is an action attached. If you wonder if you've made a strong decision, you need only to ask if there is a strong action attached?

Another way most people misunderstand decision is found in how they make them. Most people make their decisions based on their current circumstances. For example, when an opportunity arrives most people start by saying things like:

"I don't have enough time."
"I don't have enough money."
"I don't know enough."
"I don't have enough experience."

Each of these statements is based on where they feel they are now, but what they don't understand is that decision affects the future, not the present. If for example you did not have enough time, money, knowledge or experience, the only thing that would change the future would be to make a new decision in the present. More time, money, knowledge and experience all come from a new decision that is to be made prior to these things arriving.

Make a new decision, receive a new outcome.

Leap and the net will appear. - Zen Proverb

Decisions and consequences are inseparably connected. When we make a new decision, we automatically receive new outcomes.

Exercise - Consider the outcomes that you would like to create in your life. Consider the decisions that others who have achieved these outcomes before have had to make. What are some of the same decisions that you will need to make?

Exercise - Decisions are incomplete without action. Consider several of the decisions that you can make that will move you closer to your goals and desired outcomes. What actions can you take that would demonstrate your level of commitment or decision?

If you fill your day with absolute thoughts that inspire you, you create an outcome of inspiration, but if you subordinate to the world on the outside and live in the shadows of others, all of the other thoughts will create cacophony instead of a symphony out of your life, and it will make you break down with entropy instead of building you up with a vision and inspiration to transform the world. - Dr. John Demartini

If your best thinking efforts so far have gotten you to where you are now, then can that same thinking get you to where you really want to be? The answer obviously is no. So, what do we need to create even grander results? It's by actually looking at things from a different, even higher perspective. - Jason Parker

Actions

Often, we are told to take massive action. Nearly everywhere online, I have seen people telling everyone to hustle, grind, wake up early and stay up late. Unfortunately, I don't see a lot of these people telling people what to do during that time.

It's also interesting to observe a lot of the gurus of today encouraging people to take massive action. I think it's important to return to the goal of why we do what we do. I don't think it's the goal to be busy. Productivity is the goal.

As I have studied the top achievers and explored 'How' thoughts really do become things it has quickly become apparent that the goal isn't to become busy. It is to become effective, and when people are talking about the things that they wish to create in the idea of thoughts becoming things, one of the things they want is their time as well as whatever object they have set their sights on. For this simple reason alone, I think it's really important that the actions you take have a focused goal in mind.

Instead of promoting the idea of massive action, I would recommend that deliberate action is the goal.

Exercise- What deliberate actions can be taken to help you move closer to your goal and outcome?

Exercise - Who can help you identify the most effective deliberate actions you could take to get to the outcomes you desire?

Law of probability

The law of probability is something that not a lot of people have heard about. However, as I interviewed the world's top achievers, most of them understood it. The reason I am sharing it here is that I believe it is an important and essential ingredient to getting the Law of Attraction to work for you.

One of my regrets with the film How Thoughts Become Things is that we were not able to go into greater detail with this powerful principle. In fact, I believe it is one of the foundational principles required to manifest the reality that we desire, but no one is really talking about it.

Let me share first what this principle is and how it works. Then I will show you how it can work for you. The Law of Probability is not a new concept. The first mention that I can find of the Law of Probability is in a quotation from Aristotle. Aristotle wrote, "That which is probable is most likely to occur."

At first glance that idea seems pretty basic and common sense, but there is great power in this if we consider it with closer examination. The idea of proximity to your desired outcome has been repeated throughout history, but it is rarely considered in the context of personal development.

To share this example more clearly, imagine an archer standing at one side of a football field. The distance of the field is 100 yards and at the opposite end of the field is a target. Consider for a moment what would be the chances of the archer hitting a bull's-eye from a distance of a 100 yards. For most archers, it would be quite difficult.

Imagine now that the archer took a giant step forward towards the target. What would happen to his chances? Would they increase or decrease or stay the same?

Naturally, they would increase, as he was now 1 foot closer. What would happen if he took another step and then another? Of course, with each step forward, his chances of hitting the target would increase. Eventually, if he continued to step forward, he would increase the likelihood that he could shoot his arrow and hit the center of the target.

How does this relate to you manifesting your dreams and desires? Simple. As in this analogy, the closer you put yourself to the things you want to create, the more likely or probable it will be that they will occur.

So, the big question becomes, how can you increase the probability that your dream or goal can manifest itself?

There are four ways in which you can increase the probability that your desired outcome will occur.

The People You Spend Time With

You've heard it said countless times that you become like the five people you spend the most time with. This statement is important for three reasons. Firstly, we always rise to the standards of those we spend the most time with. They're the group that we gain our values from.

In fact, most people say that your network determines your net worth. Most of the time, they focus on the money part of net worth. However, I think it's also important to look at the word worth in another way. Worth = worthy, worthwhile and values. Your network also is a reflection of your net values. We gain our beliefs and values through association. When we choose our network, we are subscribing to the values of that group.

Secondly, our peers are our influences in terms of where we gain our opportunities. They open doors for us. If we are looking to manifest amazing and powerful things in our life, they will most likely arrive through others or by an introduction from someone else.

Thirdly, the people we spend time with are our safety net. I have often said that before our network determines our net worth, they are our safety net. They help us with solutions to our problems and give us insight into how to overcome challenges. If you have a low-level network, chances are very good that you are not able to solve high level problems.

Knowledge and Experience

You can increase your probability by increasing your knowledge. The more you know, the more power you have to act or to refrain from acting. Knowledge is one of the things that keeps most people from experiencing the outcomes they want, mostly because they don't know enough to recognize opportunities that appear in disguise. Without knowledge they can't see what could be or recognize the seeds of something that will be great.

The more you know, the more you can understand what you will need to do. I have had this conversation with many people in regards to investing. One of the reasons many people hold back from participation is that they feel there is too much risk involved. How do you eliminate risk? Simple. Get educated.

The more educated you are on a subject the less risky it becomes. Your education makes you an expert. You know what to look for and what to beware of. You can make effective judgements and recognize what you should walk away from.

Think of it this way. If your goal is to own a rental property and you've never done it before, you are taking a big risk if you don't get help, but if you've done 50 or 100 units prior to this time there really isn't much of a risk because you have learned so much along the way. Your experience and education have made the situation much less risky.

Geography and Where You Are

Geography refers to geographical location. There are certain locations that will improve the probability or likelihood of an event or outcome occurring. For example, if you wanted to be a movie actor, the chances of doing so would be better if you were in Los Angeles, California rather than hanging out in Mombassa, Nairobi.

Certain locations are primed to support you on your journey to your goals. The opportunities are there. The infrastructure is in place to support growth or expansion of a dream or goal. The people whom you will need are attracted to that location and so forth.

When we consider locations have a power to inspire, specific geography has power as well. Considering examples from my own life, there are certain locations which inspire a higher level of thinking and creativity than others. There are areas which are uplifting to me. Some of these locations have been the inspiration for a book, a business, a relationship and even my next movie.

Frequency and Consistency

The final and perhaps most important element of activating the Law of Probability has to do with frequency and consistency. What is meant by this is specifically how often and how consistent you are in increasing your probability through the use of the previous three elements: People, Knowledge and Geography.

How often are you meeting people who can help you?
How often are you learning about the thing you are trying to do?
How often are you going to the locations that can empower you?

Frequency and consistency are the tools which shift the ideas from your interior thinking to your tangible reality. When you are an active part of the work you are intending to create, that world begins to plant sprouts and seeds around you that change your entire environment. It could be said that not only do our thoughts become things but our proximity changes who we are and what we will experience.

Too often I hear of people who proclaim they want new outcomes and more powerful possibilities, but they remain content to hang out with the same people, learn nothing new and won't budge from their current geography. When you change nothing, nothing changes for you.

Nothing changes unless you choose to change. - Jason Parker

Think Big

Thinking big doesn't cost a penny more. The size of your thinking determines the size of your results. When we think bigger, our possibilities also expand. Thinking big is always the result of deliberate and careful thinking. No one has ever thought big by accident. You've got to decide to do so and then start thinking with purpose.

Thinking big is also a process. Often, the more you think of big ideas, the more you can build on them.

Exercise - Keep a notebook with you always and get into practice recording and expanding on ideas that you may have throughout the day. Thinking big is a habit that improves with practice. Naturally, you'll find that not all of your ideas are stellar, and some might even feel foolish. Keep writing. You'll be surprised that if you keep it up you will hit on some really good ideas from time to time, but they will only flow if you let the imperfect ones arrive as well. Don't censor yourself.

I think the biggest mistake when people are formulating their thoughts is that they think too small. They think in terms of past experiences. Most of what we're going for is based on what we think is possible. What we think is possible is based on our past experience. It's what we already tried. Somebody else tries something. We heard something, we read something, we saw on television or in a movie or in the news, and we don't stretch. We don't think big. I actually think we should be thinking so big that other people will think we're crazy when they hear our ideas. So the big mistake people make when they're thinking is just thinking too small, thinking too safe, thinking too comfortable. - Joe Vitale

How do you define a big idea? Think about that. Naturally we define big ideas based on our previous experience and the context in which the thought occurs. As most people have not had experience thinking on bigger levels, most of the time the things we label as "big thinking" are not really as big as it could be. Even though we say we are thinking big, we still hold back.

Exercise - Think about what your big thinking looks like. Then ask yourself how could I make this even bigger and more powerful? Sometimes, because we aren't used to thinking big, it can help to use our imagination to consider how someone else that we admire would think big of the same situation. Take a moment and journal about how you can start thinking big and in what ways this would be reflected in your daily life through your habits and activities.

Understand this: I don't care how good you are, you can get better, and you want to do something. The essence of who you are is wanting to get better, because that essence is perfection, that perfection seeking expression. That's why you always want to. If you're singing, you want to sing a better song. If you're running, you want to run faster. Jumping, you want to jump higher. You're selling, you want to sell more. You should never be satisfied. My grandmother pretty well raised me; she was an angel of God, but she was wrong. She said you should be satisfied. You should never be satisfied. You should be happy with whatever you've got, but you should never be satisfied. Dissatisfaction is a creative state, it's going to get you to reach higher, and if you know how to reach your goal, your goal probably isn't any good. See the real hard chargers, they're going after something, they have no idea what's gonna happen. They just know it's gonna happen. - Bob Proctor

Thinking bigger than you currently are, is the foundation of progress. You can't create better and bigger outcomes without first thinking at bigger and higher levels. Outcomes follow the spark of the thoughts we have.

If we're constantly worrying, our mind is going constantly at 100 miles an hour. We're not going to be able to hear higher guidance. If you're constantly worrying, you're severing your connection to those higher thoughts. - Jason Parker

It's interesting to point out that often you will have no idea how the things you think about will arrive. If you think this through, you'll realize that not knowing is natural and also exciting. If you already knew it, you would be able to create it without any challenges. The things you would want to manifest would be instant and sometimes you would end up creating things you actually didn't want after all.

In some ways, the journey to learn more about what we want and what is required is a safety mechanism to protect us. Often, we need to learn more about what we think we want and in the process, we can recognize how the things we think we want aren't in line with our desires and values after all.

However, there is also an exciting part about not having all of the answers. Creating and manifesting our lives becomes a journey of discovery and growth. We learn new skills, gain powerful and profound insights, and develop the ability to support those around us on their journeys.

We don't need to understand the 'how' in the beginning of the manifestation process. The 'how' will appear, but it will only appear clearly when we get committed and focused enough to start observing our environment to take advantage of 'how' moments and opportunities when they appear.

Perhaps this is another reason why having a good support network and experienced influences around us is good. We don't have to spot the 'how' moments alone. Those in our support network are there to help, and through their experience, they often can help us recognize exactly what we should do.

I do want to be clear that while you don't need to know 'How' when starting the process, it is essential to start figuring it out along the way and doing something about it when it appears. This is the difference between deliberate creation and remaining on autopilot.

Exercise - SStart talking to people who have achieved outcomes similar to what you want to create. Ask them specifically about their journey and the experience of "how' they were able to create the outcomes that they did. It's also a good idea to ask them about the challenges they experienced and how they overcame them. Keep in mind that your experiences may not unfold in the same way but having a clearer view of what possibly lies ahead will increase your ability to have correct expectations and take advantage of opportunities because you know what you're looking for.

In my personal experience, as I began a journey to interview the world's top achievers and top entrepreneurs, this exercise helped me very much. The reason why may not be what you think at first. As I shared with other top achievers what my mission was, they understood my mission. Oftentimes, they went out of their way to help me with connections to other top achievers and business leaders. These personal introductions opened more doors faster than nearly anything else I could have done.

Looking back on this experience, I have become quite convinced that manifestation happens quicker when it becomes a group effort.

Imagination

Imagination is the ability to see things in our mind. This is the beginning of seeing things in reality. We generally cannot create what we cannot see, and certainly those things which take high levels of effort require a higher level of clarity in vision.

The human mind fights against things it does not believe real or possible. When the vision or imagination cannot see something as realistic or possible, the mind will convince you to hold back your best efforts and sometimes not even try. However, when we see things vividly and powerfully, we engage with enthusiasm.

Knowledge is what we know, imagination is what we've yet to learn. - Denis Waitley

In the film there is another thought that Denis Waitley shared that is worth thinking deeply about:

Imagination rules the world. - Denis Waitley

I invite you to think carefully on this idea. Does imagination rule the world? How does it rule the world? What does that mean for you personally?

The power of imagination is often overlooked or minimized. When we consider that thoughts do indeed becomes things, the concept of imagination becomes more significant. Most people don't use their thoughts to create exciting or empowering possibilities.

Most people spend most of their thinking time in reactive or responsive ways. Imagination is truly one of the most proactive modes our thinking can shift to. It is a creative process that opens up a deliberate path to a destiny we desire.

When people talk about imagination, most think of artist endeavors or the creativity that they let go, while a young child in school. The truth is that imagination is reflected in all areas of our life and precedes all possibilities and change. When we can imagine new and thrilling choices, we have begun to create them and draw them into existence.

Many of my teachings center on creating wealth and abundance. A frequently repeated idea that I share with my students is that resourcefulness always precedes resources. It doesn't take money to make money. Money follows creativity and ideas.

This connect doesn't just work for money but works for all abundance and increase. Abundance follows imagination and resourcefulness.

Imagination is your ability to create something that you've never experienced before. It's that opportunity to become creative and generate new thought processes, new ideas, new ways of doing things than ever before. - Meagan Fettes

I love the concept of imagination being an opportunity. Imagination is also a gift. Imagination is the most powerful creative force in the universe. When we approach our lives with imagination, the events in our lives become magical.

Imagination is your mind and your heart working together to create things in your life that you will find magical. It is sometimes easy in the day-to-day grind of life to forget how these things must work together to help you find happiness. Life is a miracle! Life is marvelous!

Listen to your marvelous mind. You'll be glad you do. - Bob Proctor

This is essential advice from Bob Proctor, but there is a subtle insight here that I think is worth pointing out. Your mind always whispers to you how you should see things and what you should believe. Sometimes, it whispers doubts, fears, hesitation and undermines your confidence.

I think it's important to point out that Bob suggests we should listen to the marvelous and more powerful part of our mind. The part that supports us, encourages us, sees the best in us and wants us to experience greater success.

As we strive to listen to the more marvelous and powerful viewpoint of who we are, we will grow in our capacity to create a strong version of us. That better version of us will be able to help us create the outcomes that we desire, and our reality will change for the better.

Exercise - Make a careful effort over the next seven days to listen to only your marvelous mind. When you recognize a thought appearing, question the source. Is this your marvelous mind talking to you or is it the opposite voice. Do these whisperings which you hear have a mission to empower you or cause you to question your greatness?

Your beliefs become your thoughts,
Your thoughts become your words,
Your words become your actions,
Your actions become your habits,
Your habits become your values,
Your values become your destiny.
- Gandhi

Questions - What will you do next?
Why is authenticity important in creating outcomes?
How is a decision different than a declaration?
Why do most people make decisions incorrectly?
What important ingredient can never be left out of making a decision?
What is the difference between massive action and deliberate action?
What deliberate actions can you take today?
What is the Law of Probability?
Who could you spend more time with to get to your goals?
What could you learn more of to increase the chances of getting to your goals?
Where could you go to increase the probability of getting to your goals?
How frequently are you doing these things?
Why is thinking big important?
Why do most people not think big?
How can you encourage bigger thinking?
Why is knowing HOW when starting not necessary?
How can you enlist the help of others in the manifestation process?
Who can help you manifest the outcomes you are currently seeking?
How did these other people manifest the same outcomes that you want?
What obstacles did they encounter, and how can you prepare for the same?
How does imagination rule the world?
Why do resources follow resourcefulness?
How does imagination influence your ability to create with your thoughts?
How can you increase your ability to imagine?
What is your marvelous mind?

HOW THOUGHTS BECOME THINGS™

Let's return to the science laboratory and the question of the Law of Attraction, back to the conversation with my friend at the university. You'll remember this is where my quest began to understand what the Law of Attraction was and how it really worked. You'll remember that my professor friend stated that the Law of Attraction was not a scientific law because it did not have variables that could be applied by everyone. Hopefully as you have read this book and have seen the film, you have a sense that although the Law of Attraction may not be purely scientific, in the traditional sense, there are many things within our power.

There are many things within our own abilities and power to manifest the outcomes that we are seeking in our life. There are many influencing factors that we can choose and take action with that will allow us to produce what we really want.

If there is one thing that I learned in this journey, it is that we can choose, and when we decide to pursue specific choices, those outcomes appear. The effort to create these outcomes must be consistent and persistent. The Law of Attraction isn't one event but a series of pieces working together.

It has been refreshing to me to understand that the Law of Attraction when truly understood is not as magical or mystical as some suggest or fear. Perhaps this is one of the reasons why some people have painted the Law of Attraction in a negative light. I want to share something without sounding negative.

It has been interesting to read the comments on social media in regards to this film, my previous films and other discussions around the Law of Attraction. However, there have been some very harsh and ill-informed comments directed towards this subject matter.

First of all, it's important to not be offended when someone expresses an opinion about the Law of Attraction. Starting as a skeptic, I can understand why some of these people have felt this way. However, it is interesting to observe that they have simply not understood, nor have they taken the time to find out. For those of us who have an understanding of what the Law of Attraction is, we have a special responsibility. The Law of Attraction is a conversation of inclusion rather than exclusion.

We must expand who we are before we can see an expansion of what we have. The journey of expansion is most visible in how we think about and act towards other people. When we are kind, inclusive and supportive of others, we are most in harmony with the universe. We can literally feel the support and kindness we give others returning to us.

If you are feeling frustrated, depressed, negative or challenged in any way, the fastest way to feel better is to do something for someone else. If you want to multiply the effect of this power, do it anonymously and in secret. When we become truly concerned about the welfare of others, we expand our own well-being.

Wouldn't it be an amazing thing if more people understood just that simple message. Perhaps there is a way to grow the message and internalize it more effectively ourselves.

I recently received a letter from a lady who I will call Lisa. She had recently gone through a bitter divorce. She was experiencing financial difficulties, and as a single mother she was feeling frustrated

and challenged by all the things that seemed to be piling up on her plate. Not only was there far more to do, but everything she was doing seemed to be turning out terribly. She felt alone and depressed.

At about this time, she discovered our film How Thoughts Become Things. At first, she thought of it as simply a nice little film with a few good ideas, but there was one idea within the film that caught her attention.

The idea was that she was sending out thoughts of resentment, frustration, and victimhood regularly. In her heart she was hurt and knew that just saying "I'll think better," wouldn't work or last very long.

Within a short time, she discovered that the key wasn't to try and control her thoughts but rather re-shape her environment as we've talked about in this book. Soon, Lisa began to experience the universe in a different way. She began to look outside herself, and soon, things began to shift for the positive.

Things improved financially. She began to feel less frustrated and see that she had more power over her circumstances than she had thought possible in the beginning. As she helped others, the help she needed seemed to pour in.

Recognizing that much of what she was experiencing came directly from applying the film, she began to share it with friends. The more that she brought these concepts and strategies to the forefront in her awareness, the more she began to see them working in her life.

One of the best ways to internalize this message is to share it. I challenge you to share the message of the 'Law of Attraction' and 'How Thoughts Become Things' with others. This will benefit you in several ways.

The first is that the friend you share this with will be a great accountability partner where the two of you can support each other on your journey to manifest the future you individually desire.

Second, as you share the principles and discuss them together or in a study group you will grow in your understanding and application of the principles presented here. The more familiar you are with these concepts, the more they will become automatic and natural.

Third, as you keep these concepts at the top of your mind, you will be reminded how much power you actually have over your thoughts. When we are in a state of greater awareness, we rise from the position of autopilot and take deliberate control over our destiny, and when we do slip into moments of autopilot, which is what all humans do from time to time, our autopilot will actually be performing with intention.

Exercise - Host a watch party for the movie How Thoughts Become Things or start a study group for this book. As a side note, for those who host a watch party with 25 or more people, please drop us a note, and we can often make an arrangement for one of the teachers from the film to join you via a video call to have a Q & A or discussion about the principles discussed in the film and book. Here's my email to make arrangements and understand more about how this opportunity for you could work: doug@douglasvermeeren.com

Exercise - Now that you have read the book and hopefully seen the accompanying film, I would encourage you to take some time and consider the things that you want to manifest in your life. As you consider these things, think very carefully on the changes you will need to make to not only manifest the outcome you want, but to be able to sustain them long term. Remember at the outset of the book and film, I spoke about the importance of "Becoming."

What you choose to do next with this information will determine the value of the experience. If you simply say to yourself that this was an enjoyable experience, your journey will end there. However, if you decide that you will begin to look for ways to implement what you have learned here and make the necessary changes to apply what you have learned, this film and book will have been one of the greatest experiences in your life.

Naturally, I encourage you to seek the greatness which is within you. Seize the opportunities that are all around you every day. Rise to the higher standard and seek out the influences that will make you more of what you want to be.

And above all, remember that your thoughts do indeed, become things.

Questions - Concluding thoughts
What do you understand the Law of Attraction to be?
How is the Law of Attraction a series of events rather than just one?
How will you apply the lessons you have learned on this journey?
What elements of the Law of Attraction have you misunderstood?
What needs to happen before you can start manifesting what you desire?
How does having a correct understanding allow for better application?
How can you improve the pieces of the Law of Attraction working in your life today?
How can you help others who lack understanding?
How will you expand who you are?
How can you share the message of How Thoughts Become Things with others?
Who will you choose to become?

HOW THOUGHTS BECOME THINGS™

Douglas Vermeeren

Douglas Vermeeren has personally interviewed business leaders from companies like Nike, Reebok, Fruit of the Loom, FedEx, American Airlines, UGG boots, Uber, KFC, McDonalds, Disney, United Airlines, Ted Baker and others to share their success secrets with you. ABC television and FOX Business refer to him as the modern-day Napoleon Hill.

He is also the producer and director of four of the top ten personal development movies ever made, and now the new hit film *How Thoughts Become Things*. Douglas has authored three books in the Guerrilla Marketing series. He is a regular featured expert on FOX, CNN, ABC, NBC, CTV, CBC and others.

His training programs share strategies of how to connect with the highest-level achievers and expand your network to grow your business. His award-winning entrepreneur & wealth training programs have been rated among the best in the world.

www.DouglasVermeeren.com

Bob Proctor

Bob Proctor is a world-renowned speaker, motivational coach, author of bestselling books, as well as a Law of Attraction teacher. Bob Proctor has an international reputation for getting the very best out of both people and businesses.

Denis Waitley

Best-selling author and speaker, Denis Waitley has painted word pictures of optimism, core values, motivation and resiliency that have become indelible and legendary in their positive impact on society. He has studied and counselled leaders in every field, including Apollo astronauts, heads of state, Fortune 500 top executives, Olympic gold medalists and students of all ages and cultures.

Dr. Joe Vitale

Once homeless but now a motivating inspiration known to millions of fans as "Mr. Fire!" - is the world-renowned author of numerous best-selling books.

He is considered one of the top 50 most inspiring speakers in the world. He travels around the globe, from Iran to Russia to Italy and Poland, sharing his uplifting messages and inspiring stories.

He is also the world's first self-help singer-songwriter, with sixteen albums out and many of his songs nominated for the Post Award (considered the Grammys of positive music.)

www.vitalelifemastery.com

Dr. John Demartini

Dr. John Demartini is a world-renowned specialist in human behavior, a researcher, author and global educator. He has developed a series of solutions applicable across all markets, sectors and age groups.

His education curriculum ranges from corporate empowerment programs, financial empowerment strategies, self-development programs, relationship solutions and social transformation programs.

His teachings start at the core of the issue, addressing the human factor and range out to a multitude of powerful tools that have proven the test of time.

He has studied over 30,000 books across all the defined academic disciplines and has synthesized the wisdom of the ages which he shares on stage in over 100 countries. His presentations whether keynotes, seminars or workshops, leave clients with insights into their behavior and keys to their empowerment.

www.Drdemartini.com

John Assaraf
John has built 5-multimillion-dollar companies, written two New York Times Bestselling books and has been featured in 8 movies, including the blockbuster hit "The Secret" and "Quest For Success" with Richard Branson and the Dalai Lama.

Today, he is founder and CEO of NeuroGym, a company dedicated to using the most advanced technologies and evidence-based brain training methods to help individuals unleash their fullest potential and maximize their results.

www.JohnAssaraf.com

Marie Diamond
Marie Diamond is a globally renowned Transformational Teacher, Leader, Speaker and International Best-Selling Author, Creator of Diamond Feng Shui, Diamond Dowsing, and Inner Diamond Meditation Programs. She is also the only European star in the worldwide phenomenon "The Secret." She uses her extraordinary knowledge of Energy, Quantum Physics, the Law of Attraction, and ancient wisdom like Meditation, Feng Shui and Dowsing to support individuals, organizations and corporations to transform their success, financial situation, relationships, motivation and inspiration.

Bob Doyle
Bob Doyle is best known for his contribution to the global phenomenon, film and book "The Secret," as a Law of Attraction expert. He has been teaching these principles through programs, live events, podcasts, livestreams, coaching, writing, and even virtual reality, since 1998.

Bob is driven by his passion for creative self-expression and his work is heavily focused on helping people decide who they want to be and how they want to express themselves.

Recently, Bob's attention has shifted from the metaphysical aspects of the Law of Attraction or the "reality creation" process, to a more grounded and biological look at what controls our experiences...the wiring of our brain.

In addition to his Law of Attraction work, Bob is a serial entrepreneur, has been a voiceover artist since 1985, and is the host of The Bob Doyle Show, an "info-tainment" live program where Bob showcases his other outlets of creativity including music, computer animation, virtual reality, and more.

MeetBobDoyle.com

Jason Parker

"When are you going to grow up, get a real job and give up on this Olympic dream?" After 16 years of training and missing the Olympics for the third time, these words cut deep into Jason. Having fallen hundreds of times in his career, this time, he almost stayed down.

Just like you, Jason still had something he needed to achieve, something that was far greater than himself or even an Olympic medal. He became infatuated with the study of High Performance (and has since trained in 11 different disciplines). Then a single thought changed everything. "Maybe life isn't about achievements. Maybe life is about contribution." In that moment, everything stopped being about him, the Olympics and what he wanted to achieve. Instead, it started being about the difference he could make in the world.

Now as an Olympic Medalist, Transformational Coach, Speaker, Mastermind Leader, and leading expert in Neural Performance Language, Jason helps unfulfilled, uninspired business owners implement his "Olympian Success Formula" to become inspired, impact-driven entrepreneurs. This Formula empowers people to transcend their stuck mindsets and limiting beliefs, to unlock their own "Olympian Within".

Go to www.JasonParker.co now to OLYMPIFY your life and business today.

Dr. Travis Fox

For the last 25 years, Travis has been training and teaching his proprietary methodology Architecting sales, marketing, communication, branding and corporate cultures for both private and public corporations. Utilizing his skills for personality profiling, effective listening, focused concentration and rapport building, Travis' method has effectively helped improve corporations, entrepreneurs, and product messaging, guiding them to the heart of their message.

In addition to his television shows, and his work with the mind, Travis is also a full-fledged entertainer. He has performed his own personal brand of entertainment in over 6,500 performances worldwide over the past 25 years. At corporate events, Travis is more than just your standard speaker; he has excelled at being a Master of Ceremonies.

Dr. Marina Bruni, JD

Dr Marina Bruni is trained as a lawyer but also coaches and speaks on the power and workings of the brain. Her programs help people get results in all areas of their lives by providing a strong understanding of how the brain works. With her background in law, she is gifted at helping people see the case for developing and empowering your mind as the pathway to creating the outcomes you most want to receive.

Dr. Bruni specializes in helping entrepreneurs and small business owners to discover their greatest strengths and powers. She is a recognized leader in helping people find the path to greater personal productivity and focus.

Marina is based in London, UK. She is fluent in English, Italian and French.

www.Marinabruni.com

Meagan Fettes

Meagan, founder of RISE Yoga School, RISE Entrepreneur Center and Entrepreneur Fit, is known for teaching world-wide tools that people can use to access greater joy, abundance and success in their lives and business. She breaks down the science and fundamentals of our mind, holding patterns and vibrational shifts to support people in stepping into a higher potential and live with more fulfilling relationships and work life. Meagan's teachings come from a deep understanding of Yoga Philosophy, Universal Laws, Psychology and embodying the skills of balancing our lower and higher minds to live a life with ease, balance, and abundance.

For over 15 years, Meagan has taught and coached others how to live from a heart space and utilize the skills of visualization and manifestation to create the life they desire. She is a highly sought-after teacher and continues to share her passion while empowering others to see what is possible for them in their lives.

www.Meaganfettes.com

Dr. Karen Perkins

Dr. Karen Perkins is the "living first class KPI authority." (KPI stands for Key Performance Indicators.) For over 30 years, Dr. Perkins has worked with corporations and individuals to assess their productivity and develop a plan to improve the success ratios. She worked with these groups as a mentor, coach, advisor, and consultant. She has taught and ultimately inspired well over half a million people worldwide.

She is an engaging international speaker, executive coach, human behavioral expert, a best-selling author, a highly sought-after business leader, mentor and consultant in both the private and public sectors.

Her desire is to help others take control of their destiny and live their first-class life with their true core values. She willingly shares the secrets to this success and guides people to their path of finding their own first-class life.

www.dr-perkins.com

BOB PROCTOR | DENIS WAITLEY | JOHN DEMARTINI | JOE VITALE | DOUGLAS VERMEEREN | MARIE DIAMOND

BOB DOYLE | JOHN ASSARAF | TRAVIS FOX | JASON PARKER | MARINA BRUNI | MEAGAN FETTES

COME SEE THE MOVIE

FIND A SCREENING NEAR YOU

SEE IT ONLINE

WWW.HOWTHOUGHTSBECOMETHINGSFILM.COM

HOW THOUGHTS
BECOME THINGS™

www.ingramcontent.com/pod-product-compliance
Lightning Source LLC
Chambersburg PA
CBHW070133100426
4274CB000009B/1816